TOMBSTONE INSCRIPTIONS OF ORANGE COUNTY, VIRGINIA

I0126866

By Margaret C. Klein

With a Foreword by
William H. B. Thomas, Chairman
Orange County Bicentennial Commission

CLEARFIELD

Reprinted for
Clearfield Company, Inc. by
Genealogical Publishing Co., Inc.
Baltimore, Maryland
1992, 1995, 2001

International Standard Book Number: 0-8063-4572-1

DEDICATED

TO

VERNA BROCKHURST

without whose encouragement,
help, and support this book would never
have been completed.

PREFACE

Among the first Bicentennial projects sponsored by the Orange County Bicentennial Commission was that of recording Orange County gravestone inscriptions.
This effort was to be directed particularly to locating private or family cemeteries
and transcribing the inscriptions on markers found there. The Commission recog-
nized that through lack of care and occasional wanton destruction, information
uniquely important had already been, and would continue to be, lost forever.

Recording gravestone inscriptions is not easy work. It is a frequent neces-
sity to walk for considerable distances merely to find a cemetery, to stumble over
hidden furrows and groundhog holes, to risk poison oak or ivy, wasp stings or
snake bites. It is time-consuming and can be tedious, and worse, unrewarding - -
if, in a particular cemetery, there are no stones at all or stones without inscriptions.
It is a task that calls for devoted, determined people.

It was fortuitous, therefore, that Mrs. Alfred T. Burruss of Orange Springs,
Orange County, agreed to guide the project. More than that, she has personally done
much work in the field. Her warm interest in and very considerable knowledge of
Orange County history, particularly of the Orange Springs area, have proved to be
invaluable assets. In particular, F. O. Briggs, Jr. of Gordonsville, Virginia, has
assisted in field work and has furnished valuable data from his personal files. The
Bicentennial Commission realized at the outset, of course, that the endeavor to record gravestone inscriptions would entail long-term efforts and involve the work of
many people.

Quite independently of the Bicentennial project - indeed, unaware of its ex-
istence - and on her own initiative, Dr. Margaret Klein began an intensive program
in the spring of 1978 of recording gravestone inscriptions in the county and gathering
information concerning unmarked, but known burials. Having assembled an impressive
array of information, Dr. Klein has arranged that information in eminently usable
fashion and has provided an invaluable index. But her compilation, it should be
pointed out, does not include material furnished by the Bicentennial project.

The Bicentennial Commission recognizes, nevertheless, that Dr. Klein's
work has reached a point at which its publication will be a significant contribution
to the history of Orange County and the genealogy of its families. The Commission
welcomes, therefore, the publication of Dr. Klein's book, believing it will also
prove an inspiration to continuing effort on a truly worthy undertaking.

February 26, 1979   William H. B. Thomas
                           Chairman
                           Orange County Bicentennial Commission

TABLE OF CONTENTS

FAMILY CEMETERIES

INTRODUCTION

What seems to be long ago and yet only yesterday we began to work on the histories of our grandchildrens' families. There was a paucity of material in print for the branches of the families living at one time or another in Orange County, Virginia. Hence, this record of the tombstone inscriptions of Orange County, Virginia came into being.

The project began in earnest when Verna and Bob Brockhurst and I met one cold day in March 1978 at Zoar Baptist Church Cemetery and realized we were functioning on the same wave-length. We made inquiries at the courthouse in Orange, at the Orange Public Library, at the State Library in Richmond, and at the DAR Library in Washington, D.C. Every response was the same: "No records". As we continued to search for our own grandchildrens' ancestors, we became very much aware of the wealth of unrecorded information in the cemeteries. We retraced our steps, obtained old maps and new ones, and began to search and record, not only for ourselves, but for others.

Since I reside in Orange County and write a genealogy column for the ORANGE COUNTY REVIEW, I appealed to my readers for help in locating the older, forgotten cemeteries. Several answers were submitted, some without the name of the writer, others very well documented with much family history included. The field work was accomplished during the summer. My thanks go out to Verna and Bob Brockhurst for their assistance in recording the larger cemeteries. At Graham, a team of friends — Eleanor Hearn, Agnes Kirby, the Brockhursts — and I copied all of the stones.

I visited the local funeral homes and had complete cooperation from the funeral directors. They were able to tell me about small cemeteries, identify them by surname, and in some cases point out cemeteries we had missed entirely. Only recently Mr. Tony Preddy, director of Preddy's Funeral Home in Orange, has opened his older logs to us to verify some of our information. The logs would supply many additional names and cemeteries.

There were visits with post office personnel which yielded information on the location of some cemeteries, and talks with gentlemen at local stores that proved productive. By the end of the summer we were "door-knocking" at every likely-looking home. We had exhausted most of the information on our USGS maps by then. Through our door-knocking we discovered that a similar project had been begun by the Orange County Bicentennial Commission. We want to thank Mr. William H.B. Thomas, Chairman of the Commission, for his support and assistance. Mrs. Alfred T. Burruss and Mr. Ferol Briggs, Jr., who had worked on that project, gave us leads and helped us in furthering our project.

Editing the multitude of names, dates and other information was time
consuming. At first it was decided to include in the book only those inscriptions
of persons who died before 1900. Quickly it became apparent that the people   of
Orange County were long-lived and that such a cut-off date would eliminate many of
the very people we wanted to include.

We re-edited and included all those who were born before 1850. That
was a much more workable date since it included most of the Civil War participants,
which in this area is most important. Orange County encompasses the Wilderness
Battlefield and is very near Chancellorsville, Spotsylvania Courthouse and other
important battlefields. We included spouses and children where it seemed appropri-
ate, and, of course, all family cemeteries.

Our thanks go out to all of the interesting and helpful people in Orange
County who so graciously opened our way by permitting us to copy the inscriptions
from graves on their property. We also want to thank those who gave us leads as
to the location of cemeteries on their homeplaces, which were often farm cemeteries
no longer accessible by vehicle. Many of the lovely ladies of Orange County invited
us to tour their homes and gardens, so that it seemed like house and garden week
every day that we went out in the field. Farmers, hunters, storekeepers, everyone
with whom we came in contact was interested and helpful. We were never refused
admittance and we were encouraged in the recording, for nearly everyone realized
the true worth of the information.

Special thanks go to Clement Bounds, who helped us locate maps; to my
husband, Rich Klein, and son Richard, who both helped with proof-reading. Of
course, my thanks go to Sarah Jeanne and Laura Xan Klein, my two granddaughters
who started all of this.

It is obvious that we have barely scratched the surface of the many small
cemeteries and hope that those of you who read this work will let us know if you find
your cemetery missing. There is a small area along the Rapidan where Kemper's
grave is located that we were never able to research, and a pocket here and there
which for one reason or another was skipped. If you send us directions, or if you
copy the information, we will be glad to include it in a later volume.

We know there may be errors in typing, recording, or even in the original
stone cutting. We have proof-read carefully, but apologize in advance for any of the
human errors that might have been avoided. We hope that this volume will begin to
fill the void in the history of this important Virginia county. We are continuing to
seek Sarah and Xan's ancestors, and perhaps their history will be completed in
the future.

1 March 1979   M.C.K.
Locust Grove, Virginia

MEMORIALS
***

WADDEL MEMORIAL

DIRECTIONS: Route 15 North from Gordonsville 0.5 miles on
left. There is a Highway Historical Marker as
well as the memorial stone.

WADDEL, James 1739 - 1825

MONUMENT TO CIVIL WAR SOLDIERS

DIRECTIONS: See MAPLEWOOD CEMETERY

UNKNOWN CONFEDERATE SOLDIERS

DIRECTIONS: See GRAHAM CEMETERY

PROPRIETARY CEMETERIES

***

GRAHAM CEMETERY

DIRECTIONS: From Orange Court House West on Route 20 for
1.0 miles to cemetery on right.

UNKNOWN CONFEDERATE SOLDIERS: Around 21 December 1978 the Thirteenth
Virginia Regiment Chapter, United Daughters of the
Confederacy obtained and had erected fifteen headstones
for unknown CSA soldiers. Caretaker Boots Davis related that long ago he was told by an elderly gentleman
that there were 15 soldiers buried in that plot. The
graves were extra long, but had been dug by a mule
and pan. The old gentleman related that he had seen
a wagon pull up and place the fifteen bodies covered
by canvas, but without coffins, placed in the graves.
Photographs of an individual tombstone and of the
dedication ceremony appear in the ORANGE COUNTY
REVIEW published 21 December 1978.

ALLEN, Archibald Oden 6 May 1862 – 9 Sept 1898 with Philip H. and Mary O. Fry
Elizabeth 1827 – 1906

AMOS, Benjamin Jefferson 15 Oct 1839 – 3 Feb 1921 husb of Bettie
Bettie 21 Dec 1839 – 19 Apr 1926 wife of Benjamin J.
George A. 5 Nov 1822 – 15 May 1903 husb of Giney D.
Giney D. 24 Nov 1834 – 4 Oct 1905 wife of George A.
John Robert 22 Nov 1867 – 25 Nov 1897
S. J. (Mrs.) no dates with W.J.
Tempie (Mrs.) 26 Nov 1804 – 28 Dec 1885 mother
W.J. no dates with Mrs. S.J.Amos

ANDREWS, Mary E. 1 Jan 1806 – 6 Aug 1869 wife of Wm H., mother of Mary Isabella
Mary Isabella 15 Mar 1838 – 13 Sept 1874 dau of Wm H. and Mary E. Andrews

ASHBY, Buckner G. 3 Dec 1834 – 5 Feb 1901

ATKINS, Patsy ... see FARRAR

AVERETT, Jesse Jr Wounded 6 May in Battle of the Wilderness, d. 12 June 1864
33 years of life

AVERILL, Susan Harriett 29 July 1845 – 26 Dec 1922

BALLARD, Garland 13 June 1798 – 25 June 1852 husb of Georgiana
Georgiana Blair March 1838 – Oct 1891
Georgiana 24 Feb 1801 – 18 Apr 1883 wife of Garland
Mary ... see HANSBROUGH

BANKHEAD, Charles Lewis 22 June 1833 – 19 Aug 1902 with Mary W.
Mary Warner 26 Nov 1831 – 3 Aug 1907 with Charles L.

BANKS, Cornelia Burnett 1853 – 1932 wife of James W.
James W. 1849 – 1938 husb of Cornelia B.

BANKS, Roberta ... see WILLIAMS

BATES, Martha A. 16 Aug 1837 - 4 Aug 1917 wife of William A.
    William A. 19 Jan 1834 - 30 Dec 1901 husb of Martha A.

BEALE, Harriet ... see GRYMES

BELL, Mary T. 22 Mar 1840 - 4 Mar 1919

BERKELEY, Henry Robinson 27 Mar 1840 - 16 Jan 1918 husb of Nannie L.
    Nannie L. 8 May 1845 - 7 Mar 1898 wife of Henry R.

BLAIR, Georgiana ... see BALLARD

BLAKEY, Ann Maria ... see NEWMAN

BLEDSOE, Bennett 25 Nov 1848 - 5 Mar 1922
    Lucy D. 6 Dec 1844 - 5 May 1916

BOND, John 1816 - 1875 husb of Lucy T.
    Lucy Tatum 1833 - 1919 wife of John
    Mary G. 5 Nov 1842 - 17 Apr 1915 with R.H.
    R. H. 22 Nov 1837 - 23 Feb 1924 with Mary G.
    Thomas W. 29 Mar 1826 - 26 Dec 1903 77 yr with Virginia W. on obelisk
    Virginia W. 22 Feb 1827 - 8 Mar 1908 with Thomas W. on obelisk

BOOTON, Mary Catlett 2 Nov 1869 - 2 July 1889
    Mildred Pendleton Williams 17 Feb 1839 - 12 Apr 1912 wife of Richard Sinclair
                                                                    Booton
    R. Sinclair 2 July 1830 - 2 Feb 1883 husb of Mildred P.W.
    William Sinclair 21 Oct 1876 - 25 July 1897

BOSWELL, C. H. 1847 - 1894
    Mary L. 4 Apr 1820 - 8 Dec 1899 with Wm J.
    Sallie M. 1845 - 1915 with C.H.
    William J. 16 Aug 1819 - 29 Mar 1896 with Mary L.

BRADBURY, Fannie Standard ... see GRYMES

BRADFORD, John E. 1822 - 1910
    Virginia F. 1825 - 1910
    William S. 1816 - 1898

BRADLEY, Lizzie B. 26 Apr 1847 - 7 May 1921
    Lucy Willis Taliaferro 23 July 1814 - 14 Sept 1902 wife of Edwin B. Bradley

BRAXTON, Bettie ... see GRYMES

BRENT, Sarah d. 12 Nov 1861 in 41st year of her age wife of Alexander Daley

BRIDWELL, Oswald H. 9 Oct 1843 - 11 Apr 1926 'husb of Sallie E.
    Sallie E. 9 Jan 1846 - 30 June 1915 wife of Oswald H.

BROWN, James Stephenson d. 14 Dec 1886 72 years of age

BROWNING, G. Judson 16 May 1830 - 9 Apr 1885 husb of Sarah Thomas
    Sarah Thomas 27 Apr 1835 - 17 June 1910 wife of G. Judson Browning

BUCKNER, Caldwell Calhoun 9 Feb 1829 - 22 May 1898

BURDETTE, Willis 16 Sept 1883 - 1 June 1898

BURGESS, Anna W.L.Taylor 16 June 1866 - 15 Aug 1954 dau of Erasmus and
                                    Roberta Taylor, wife of Wm Wallace Burgess

BURGESS, William W. jr 1 Sept 1903 - 16 Jan 1946 son of Wm Wallace and Anna
　　　　Taylor Burgess
　　William Wallace 22 June 1841 - 26 Sept 1913 son of Thomas and Honor Burgess,
　　　　husb of Anna W.L.Taylor, father of William W. jr.

BURNETT, Cornelia ... see BANKS

BURRUS, John 9 Sept 1845 - 6 Nov 1930

BUTLER, Alexandria 30 Nov 1849 - 17 Apr 1926 with Eliza Jane
　　Charlotte Langhorne ... see MADDUX
　　Eliza Jane 11 July 1857 - 30 Oct 1954 with Alexandria

CALDWELL, Maggie ... see HUME

CAMPER, Mary Christian 16 [?18?] Oct 1844 - 16 July 1923 with Rev. Wm H.
　　　　on Camper obelisk
　　William [Rev.] 18 July 1836 - 29 Jan 1917 with Mary C. on Camper obelisk

CARPENTER, Frances J. 1851 - 1934 wife of R.E.
　　R. E. 1848 - 1939 husb of Frances J.
　　Sarah E. ... see POWELL

CARTER, Ann ... see GOSS
　　Anne ... see WALKER

CATLETT, Kate ... see GRIMES
　　Mary ... see BOOTON

CHAPMAN, Mary Stanard d. 1912 wife of William Henry Chapman

CHILDRESS, Giles R. 30 Dec 1847 - 1 Sept 1939 father, husb of Sallie J.
　　Sallie J. 9 Jan 1855 - 11 Aug 1902 wife of Giles R.

CHRISTIAN, Mary ... see CAMPER

CLARK, Kennie 16 May 1852 - 1 Oct 1855 son of Francis R. and Helen M. Carr
　　　　Clark of Mobile

CLAYTON, Nannie ... see GRYMES

COLEMAN, Camilta ... see REEDY

COLLINS, Anne Elizabeth ... see PAYNE

CONWAY, Nellie ... see WILLIS

COPPAGE, Mary D. d. 1 Apr 1902 age 72 years mother

COWHERD, Powell H. 1838 - 1912 CSA

CRENSHAW, Ines Cusachs 23 June 1870 - 26 Nov 1964 wife of Wm G. jr
　　William G. jr 14 Nov 1848 - 24 Mar 1918 husb of Ines C.

CULLEN, Barbara d. 18 Dec 1899 age 84 years wife of George E.
　　George Evans d. May 1863 age 76 years husb of Barbara

CUNNINGHAM, Julia 18 Aug 1847 - 24 Feb 1917 wife of William F.
　　William F. 15 July 1847 - 16 Sept 1935 husb of Julia

CUSACHS, Ines ... see CRENSHAW
　　Louise C. 1848 - 1944

DABNEY, Tyree J. 1850 - 1907

DALEY, H. W. d. 9 July 1852 1 year with John S. and Sarah Daley
    John S. d. 15 June _____ [old, unable to read] husb of Sarah
    Sarah weathered. With H.W. and John S.
    Sarah Brent ... see BRENT

DANIEL, Matilda Willeroy d 19 Dec 1906 72 years

DAVIS, Mary W. ... see MARSHALL
    Octavia ... see NELSON

DENNIS, James M. Co A 19 Va Inf CSA no dates

DICKENSON, Florence ... see TERRILL

DOBYNS, Patsy Jean 2 Jan 1850 – 3 Jan 1950 mother

DUNN, Laura Jane Sale 19 Mar 1856 – 3 Aug 1898 wife of Wm H.

ECKLOFF, Josephine E. 1839 – 1881 on back of stone with Mary L. [R.G.
                Eckloff stone]
    Mary L. 1864 – 1866 on back of R.G. Eckloff stone
    R.G. 1833 – 1878

ELEAR, Helen 27 Dec 1771 – 10 June 1817 [very weathered stone, difficult to
            read, beside James Robinson]

ESKEW, Mary Frances 1828 – 1908 mother, wife of Wm J.
    Walter J. 1862 – 1881 son of Wm J. and Mary F. Eskew
    William J. 1829 – 1903 father, husb of Mary F.

ESTES, Annie Cordelia 13 Aug 1858 – 5 Apr 1900 wife of J.H.
    Joseph Hamet 19 Jan 1857 – 12 Aug 1946 husb of 1] Annie C. and 2] Sallie
                Minor
    Julia G. 2 June 1850 – 12 Sept 1930
    Sallie Minor 20 June 1858 – 2 Dec 1918 2nd wife of J.H.
FARRAR, Florida ... see TIGNOR
FARRER, Martha Matilda 11 Mar 1844 – 13 Oct 1924 wife of Robert James
    Patsy Atkins 7 May 1830 – 29 Mar 1916
    Robert James 6 Apr 1844 – 26 June 1916 born in Yorkshire, England died at
            his home Rounlon in Orange, Virginia husb of Martha M.

FAULCONER, Erasmus G. 23 Dec 1849 – 10 May 1930 father, husb of Mattie J.
    Mattie J. 17 Mar 1854 – 23 Jan 1930 wife of Erasmus G.

FOX, John T. b. in Fairfax 1834 – 9 Mar 1912

FRANKLIN, Charlotte ... see TALIAFERRO

FRY, Mary O. 26 Dec 1838 – 18 Sept 1925 wife of Philip H. See also ALLEN.
    Philip Henry 30 June 1834 – 21 Mar 1911 husb of Mary O.

GAINES, Andrew 28 Jan 1806 – 22 Nov 1853
    Andrew B. 24 Jan 1854 – 22 Oct 1888
    Frances Lee 12 Aug 1844 – 28 Mar 1874
    George A. 20 July 1849 – 31 Dec 1909

GARDNER, Mary Ella 21 Sept 1848 – 13 Dec 1881 wife of James Monroe Gardner

GARNETT, Jesse W. 1870 – 1906 with Martha C.
    Luther L. 1861 – 1865
    Martha C. 1828 – 1909 with Jesse W.
    Mary E. 1857 – 1869
    Robert C. 1820 – 1873
    Willis D. 1855 – 1857

GARRETT, _____   ... see HUNDLEY

GARTH, Martha 1780 - 1875

GENTRY, Bettie E. 22 Sept 1853 - 20 Apr 1933 wife of Charles H.
    Charles H. 20 July 1844 - 26 Aug 1920 father, husb of Bettie E.

GIBSON, Ammarilous ... see HERRING
    Joseph M. 28 May 1848 - 31 Dec 1932
    Linnes Churchill 12 Sept 1841 - 29 Mar 1917 CSA
    Nettie J. 12 Nov 1868 - 3 Mar 1936 wife of William E.
    William d. 1899 age 6 months son of W. E. and N. J. Gibson
    William Edward 17 Mar 1856 - 16 Aug 1939 father, husb of Nettie J.

GILLUM, Sallie Mundy 15 Dec 1855 - 5 Apr 1937 wife of Thaddeus O.
    Thaddeus Oscar 19 Oct 1849 - 19 Jan 1929 husb of Sallie E. Mundy

GIPSON, Benjamin Franklin 1846 - 1899

GODWIN, Charles 5 Apr 1830 - 29 Apr 1888

GOLSAN, Charlotte Belle no dates with Edward N.
    Edward Nalle d. 11 Oct 1884 with Charlotte B.
    Eustace F. 1843 - 1937

GOSNELL, Lydia ... see SELBY

GOSS, Ann Carter 1824 - 1907 wife of Ebenezer
    Ebenezer 1820 - 1885 husb of Ann C.
    Mary Botts 1858 - 1881 dau of E. and A.C. Goss

GRAHAM, David native of Tyronne County, Ireland d. 15 July 1870
    Lizzie Cullen 19 July 1852 - 27 May 1904 with William
    Mary Waterman d. 14 Oct 1895 wife of Robert N. Graham
    William 22 Feb 1847 - 10 May 1915 with Lizzie C.

GRASTY, John Thomas 18 Mar 1847 - 24 Oct 1901 husb of Mary Eliz. S.
    Mary Elizabeth Sale 12 Apr 1846 - 1 Feb 1915 wife of John T.

GRAVES, Francis Edward 27 Mar 1825 - 23 Jan 1899 husb of Mary P.H.
    Joseph W. C. 1 June 1844 - 5 Oct 1924 CSA [in Coleman plot]
    Mary Peach Hamilton 3 May 1830 - 2 June 1917 wife of Francis E.
    Mary Virginia ... see PARRAN
    Susan Catherine ... see SCOTT
    Ursula Kendall d. 2 June 1900 age 72 years and 8 months
    Wilhelmina G. Welch 9 June 1830 - 27 June 1901

GRAY, Fannie ... see GRYMES

GRIMES, Kate Catlett d. 1 May 1889 wife of Peyton
    Peyton d. 1 Feb 1894   husb of Kate Catlett

GRYMES, Benjamin 1856 - 1882
    Benjamin Andrew 1824 - 1884 husb of Harriet B.
    Bettie Braxton d. 12 Aug 1883
    Edward Beale 17 Sept 1860 - 29 May 1934 husb of Fannie G.
    Fannie Gray d. 2 June 1897 age 37 years wife of Edward B.
    Fannie Stanard Bradbury 12 May 1884 - 1 Feb 1961 wife of John Randolph
                Grymes
    Harriet Beale 1828 - 1912 wife of Benjamin Andrew
    Louis Bull d. 17 Nov 1885 husb of Fannie S.B.
    Nannie Clayton d. 11 Sept 1897
    Sadie ... see MONCURE

HALSEY, Eloise Rice Walker 23 Aug 1857 - 9 Dec 1916 with R. Ogden Halsey [A
        second stone with same dates has name "Ella Rice"]
    Fannie Rice 2 Jan 1877 - 31 July 1899 dau of R.O. and E.R. Halsey
    Joseph J. 5 Apr 1823 - 25 Feb 1907 husb of Mildred J.M.
    Mildred J. Morton 22 Nov 1825 - 25 Apr 1906 wife of Joseph J.
    R. Ogden 31 Oct 1854 - 15 Oct 1939 husb of Eloise R.W.

HAMILTON, Mary Peach ... see GRAVES

HAMM, Francis S. 28 Mar 1884 - 28 June 1885
    Jesse Buel 25 Dec 1851 - 27 Feb 1929 husb of Susan G.
    Olga B. 28 Feb 1881 - 15 Mar 1882
    Susan G. 3 May 1844 - 17 Sept 1907 wife of Jesse B.

HAMMOND, Henry R. 27 Oct 1826 - 29 June 1882

HANSBROUGH, John Strother 1831 - 1921 husb of Mary B.
    Mary Ballard 1833 - 1912 wife of John S.
    Mary Elizabeth 11 Apr 1860 - 4 Oct 1862

HARLIN, Mary S. ... see HARNSBERGER

HARLOW, James C. no dates Co A 23 Va Inf CSA

HARNSBERGER, John William 15 Jan 1849 - 17 Jan 1913 husb of Mary S.H.
    Mary S. Harlin 11 Mar 1850 - 16 Mar 1929

HARRISON, Nannie ... see SPARKS

HATCHER, Gillie Frances Jones 7 Apr 1839 - 29 Jan 1935 wife of Rev. Hillary E.
    Gillie Frances 26 Feb 1897 - 18 July 1897 dau of Eugene P. and Frances C.
    Hillary E. [Rev.] 8 Nov 1832 - 20 Aug 1892 husb of Gillie F.J.

HENDRICKS, C. P. 26 Jan 1850 - 5 May 1888 husb of Margaret N.
    Charles Plumb 2 Aug 1828 - 3 Jan 1899 born Yazoo County, Mississippi died
        Somerset, Orange, Virginia husb of Margaret Davis,
        Capt in Miles Legion 1st La Vol CSA
    M. N. 8 Dec 1872 - 21 Jan 1873 inf dau of C.P. and Margaret N. Hendricks
    Margaret N.   26 Jan 1850 - 5 May 1888 wife of C.P.

HERRING, Ammarilous Gibson 3 May 1860 - 6 Sept 1915 wife of Franklin T.
    Franklin Towles 23 Mar 1844 - 30 Oct 1901 husb of A.G.

HIDEN, Henry sr   22 Apr 1810 - 24 July 1866 husb of Mary
    Mary 25 May 1822 - 3 May 1882

HIGGINS, George W. 1843 - 1914

HOUSEWORTH, Harriet M. no dates wife of Joseph H.
    Joseph H. 29 Aug 1834 - 13 Mar 1896husb of Harriet M.
    Mary E. 20 Aug 1836 - 4 Feb 1904 wife of B.H. Houseworth
    Mary Martha 13 Dec 1844 - 28 Feb 1914 wife of V.A.
    Sarah Brent 24 Dec 1864 - 23 Mar 1866
    V.A. 21 Mar 1831 - 17 Jan 1908 husb of Mary M.

HUBBARD, Daniel 1817 - 1896 husb of Mary K.
    David M. 1804 - 1884
    Eugene Winthrop 1895 - 1897
    Lydia C. 1819 - 1894
    Mary K. 1820 - 1892 wife of Daniel
    Oliver 1896 - 1897

HUGHES, Nannie 1850 - 1935

HUME, Benjamin Wesley 1840 - 1915 husb of Maggie C.
    Maggie Caldwell 1840 - 1921 wife of Benjamin W.

HUNDLEY, _____Garrett 3 Mar 1832 - 16 Jan 1910 mother

HUNTON, Inez ... see PARKER

HURKAMP, Alice ... see WARREN

HUTCHISON, Bradshaw Clarkson 24 Jan 1890 - 23 Dec 1940 same stone as Bula L.,
                 Helen G., Maude, and Robert L.
    Bula Lewis 7 Oct 1892 - 25 Dec 1915 see above
    Christopher 20 Nov 1830 - 11 Apr 1881 born in England husb of Elizabeth
    Elizabeth d. 14 Jan 1915 78 years wife of Christopher
    Helen Garret 17 Jan 1851 - 9 Sept 1921 wife of Robert L. see Bradshaw C.
    Maude 27 Sept 1877 - 2 Apr 1968 see Bradshaw C.
    Robert Leachman 8 Sept 1842 - 21 May 1912 see Bradshaw C., husb of Helen

JACKSON, William 25 Apr 1842 - 13 Oct 1913

JACOBS, Alice Blanche 19 Feb 1855 - 11 Apr 1926 mother, wife of J. W.
    J. Wallace 14 Sept 1848 - 9 Mar 1933 husb of Alice B.
    John Francis 28 June 1845 - 5 June 1921
    Mary V. 1858 - 1899

JAFFRAY, Florence ... see WOODRIFF

JERDONE, Frank 8 Nov 1846 - 2 May 1923 husb of Talitha C.
    Talitha Catherine 20 May 1850 - 5 Sept 1926 wife of Frank, mother

JOHNSON, Elmira E. 12 Mar 1831 - 6 Feb 1869 wife of Joseph H.
    Evelyn ... see WILLIAMS
    Fannie 9 July 1865 - 5 May 1868 dau of J.H. and E.E. Johnson
    Joseph Henry 1 Mar 1827 - 23 May 1893 father, husb of Elmira E.
    Lelia ... see SANFORD
    Wallace 12 Mar 1859 - 14 Jan 1860 son of J.H. and E.E.

JONES, Edmonia Pilcher 18 Dec 1847 - 28 Mar 1930 wife of John E. Jones
    Gillie Frances ... see HATCHER

KENDALL, Ursula ... see GRAVES

KIBLER, Eliza A. 14 July 1845 - 27 Dec 1927 with John H.
    John H. 26 July 1844 - 21 Mar 1901 with Eliza A.

KINZER, Eunice J. 17 Aug 1827 - 23 June 1865 1st wife of John H.
    John H. 9 June 1823 - 13 Nov 1904 husb of 1] Eunice J. and 2] Susan C.
    Susan C. 31 Oct 1828 - 20 Sept 1910 2nd wife of John H.

LEE, Frances ... see GAINES

LEWIS, Annie ... see MONCURE

LIPSCOMB, Charlie D. 26 June 1869
    Claborn 4 Oct 1854 - 3 Nov 1854
    Harry E. 27 June 1871 - 1 May 1903
    J. Thomas 25 May 1866 - 17 May 1903
    John 20 June 1860 - 2 Oct 1861
    Lizzie G. 2 Apr 1872 - 4 Aug 1872
    Mary E. 24 Oct 1855
    Miles B. 3 Apr 1825 - 3 Aug 1877
    Millie B. 1 Feb 1857 - 3 Aug 1877
    Octavia M. 15 Oct 1831
    Rich W. 8 Nov 1860

LIPSCOMB, Robert M. 27 Aug 1852 - 5 Mar 1904
    Rosa L. 1 June 1875 - 23 July 1875
    Virginia L. 10 Aug 1863 - 13 July 1893

MACON, Emma Cassandra Riely 1 Oct 1847 - 13 Jan 1942 wife of Reuben C., dau
    of James Purvis and Catherine Brent Riely
    Reuben Conway 14 May 1838 - 21 Mar 1948 husb of Emma C. son of James
    Madison and Lucetta Todd Newman Macon 13th Va CSA

MADDUX, Charlotte Langhorne Butler Dec 1863 - 17 Apr 1921 wife of Clifford
    Clifford Bartlett 12 June 1851 - 13 Oct 1926 husb of Charlotte
    Marie 16 Apr 1888 - 29 June 1898 dau of Clifford and Charlotte

MARQUIS, Martha G. 9 Mar 1833 - 18 Sept 1915 wife of Walter A.
    Walter Albert 1830 - 1912 father, husb of Martha G.

MARSHALL, Annie L. 9 Mar 1877 - 3 Aug 1894
    Fielding Lewis 29 Mar 1819 - 30 June 1932
    Mary Newton 9 Aug 1842 - 4 Aug 1928
    Mary W. Davis 1844 - 1939 mother, with Winfield N.
    Winfield N. 1844 - 1887 father, Mason

MARTIN, Mary B. 14 Mar 1843 - 8 Mar 1917

MAY, Mary Francis ... see WATSON

McDONALD, John 29 Nov 1829 - 22 May 1918 with Mettie and Marshall C.
    Marshall C. 7 May 1859 - 29 Aug 1861 with John and Mettie
    Mettie 15 Sept 1833 - 21 Nov 1870 with John and Marshall C.

McINTOSH, Ebbie Frank 6 Mar 1859 - 14 Oct 1937 husb of 1] Myra N., 2] Mary E.,
    snf 3] Nancy
    Infant sons of Ebbie and Nancy no dates
    Mary Eliza Perry 10 Nov 1870 - 11 Oct 1960 wife of Ebbie F.
    Myra N. 11 Sept 1862 - 10 June 1888 wife of E.F.McIntosh
    Phyllis 4 June 1899 - 5 June 1899 dau of E.F. and M.E. McIntosh

McVEIGH, Martha A. ... see RAWLINGS

MILLER, A. J. d. 2 Apr 1903 72 years

MINOR, Sallie ... see ESTES

MONCURE, Annie Lewis Aug 1820 - 14 Nov 1905. wife of Chas. P.
    Charles Proser 1820 - 6 Jan 1887 born in Stafford County, Virginia, husb of
    Annie L.
    Elizabeth Randolph 5 Dec 1890 - 5 May 1893 child of P.V.D. and S.G.
    Henry no dates child of C.P. and A.L. Moncure
    Peter V.D. 16 Jan 1853 - 27 Jan 1931 husb of Sadie G.
    Sadie Grymes 27 Sept 1865 - 4 Nov 1952 wife of Peter V.D.Moncure

MOORE, James Mordecai 7 Mar 1842 - 14 Nov 1909
    James Stapleton 31 Mar 1849 - 23 Aug 1940 husb of Virginia M.S.
    Virginia Margaret Sale 29 Oct 1854 - 23 July 1922 wife of James S.
    Willmonia Endora 17 Feb 1843 - 2 Feb 1927

MORRIS, Ann Louisa 15 July 1834 - 28 Jan 1864 wife of Milton
    Fenton 24 June 1870 - 17 July 1870
    J.E. sr 4 July 1811 - 20 Jan 1910
    Lula 29 July 1877 - 23 Aug 1877
    Milton 17 May 1839 - 16 Nov 1859 husb of Ann L.

MORTON, Alice H. 26 Jan 1881 - 28 Aug 1892
    Emily D. 1855 - 1911 wife of James W.

MORTON, J. Kemper 6 Dec 1889 – 16 Oct 1890
James W. 1845 – 1913 husb of Emily D.
Lucy P. 22 Jan 1878 – 17 Sept 1892
Mildred J. ... see HALSEY

MUNDY, Sallie ... see GILLUM

NALLE, Lucy Mary ... see WILLIS

NELSON, Eleanor Taliaferro 1846 – 1926 mother
Octavia Davis 1830 – 1918 with R. Lewis Nelson
R. Lewis 1830 – 1900 husb of Octavia D.

NEWMAN, Ann Marie Blakey 25 Apr 1830 – 30 Dec 1915 wife of John F. in Kite
plot which is hedged
Bettie B. ... see STOVIN
Lucetta Todd ... see MACON
Mary ... see MARSHALL

NEY, Nannie 13 Mar 1840 – 22 Oct 1914 born in Ireland

NOTTINGHAM, Sally B. 1850 – 1941

ODEN, Lewis Thomas 24 Jan 1829 – 19 Feb 1898

PARKER, Alice ... see WAMBERSIE
George Samuel 10 Dec 1841 – 24 Sept 1910 husb of Inez H.
Inez Hunton d. 11 Apr 1904 wife of George S., loving sister

PARRAN, Mary Virginia Graves 1 Sept 1837 – 2 Dec 1928 wife of Dr William Sell-
man Parran, in Coleman plot
William Sellman [M.D.] 19 Mar 1863 – 21 Nov 1897 husb of Mary V.G., in
Coleman plot

PAYNE, Anne Elizabeth Collins 23 Sept 1846 – 19 July 1933 wife of Benjamin C.
Payne

PERRY, Archibald d. 17 July 1894 age 2 months and 9 days son of Levi and Julia
Perry
Julia A. Mundy 2 Feb 1852 – 14 Apr 1932 mother, wife of Levi L. Perry
Julia A. 3 Mar 1881 – 6 Jan 1898 "Little Sister"
Levi L. d. 3 Jan 1890 age 42 years 26 days husb of Julia A.M.
Maude 14 July 1876 – 11 July 1877 dau of Levi L. and Julia A. Perry
Robert Lee 10 Nov 1869 – 25 Aug 1870 son of Levi L. and Julia A. Perry
Rudolph 25 Feb 1873 – 24 Oct 1873 son of Levi L. and Julia A. Perry
Sleeping Children d. 25 June 1890 son and dau of Levi L. and Julia A. Perry

PEYTON, Sallie B. 1835 – 1913 wife of Thomas J., in Ashton plot
Thomas J. 1833 – 1910 CSA husb of Sallie B., in Ashton plot

PILCHER, Edmonia ... see JONES

POWELL, Sarah E. Carpenter 27 Mar 1835 – 13 Sept 1924 wife of W.N. Powell

PRICE, Walter Evan esq. 22 Aug 1862 – 1 July 1887 24 years "eldest son of Capt.
David Price of Clanmorlais Carmarthenshire, South
Wales"

QUESENBERRY, A.B. [Mrs.] 20 Aug 1838 – 31 Aug 1924
Vivian [Dr.] 21 June 1832 – 17 Mar 1888 died in Hinton, West Virginia

RAWLINGS, Benjamin sr. 20 Aug 1815 – 19 Feb 1894 husb of Martha A. McVeigh
Martha A. McVeigh 22 July 1827 – 8 Feb 1900 wife of Benjamin sr.
Zachariah Herndon 18 Jan 1863 – 22 Feb 1894 3rd son of Benj and Martha

REEDY, Camilta Coleman 7 Feb 1864 – 5 June 1934 wife of John A.
    John A. 12 Feb 1848 – 13 Apr 1931 husb of Camilita C.

REID, Eliza Ellen 6 Oct 1828 – 7 June 1920 wife of Hiram G.
    Hiram G. 12 July 1800-_____ husb of Eliza E. [date of death not given]
    Sheldon A. 23 Mar 1866 – 17 Aug 1898

RICE, Ella ... see HALSEY, Eloise

RICHARDSON, Anne Yeates 10 Oct 1858 – 18 July 1892 wife of George D.
    Barbara Cullen 16 Feb 1890 – 11 Sept 1890 dau of George D. and Anne Y.
    George Dudley 28 Mar 1845 – 28 Apr 1891 husb of Anne Y.
    Emma C. 20 Apr 1839 – 31 Jan 1928 wife of Wm H.
    William H. 9 Sept 1838 – 14 Feb 1909 husb of Emma C.

RIELY, Emma Cassandra ... see Macon

ROBERTS, Fannie Robertson 22 Aug 1832 – 28 Dec 1914 wife of John A. Roberts
    Lucy M. 1825 – 1920 wife of Pleasant D., mother of Roger Q., Thomas J.,
                and Joseph P.
    Pleasant D. 1825 – 1908 husb of Lucy M. "Dear Pa"

ROBERTSON, Fannie ... see ROBERTS

ROBINSON, James 20 Aug 1835 – 21 Apr 1861 beside Helen Elear
    Maria L. 28 Apr 1812 – 15 Feb 1850 consort of Thomas A., beside James
                Robinson and Halen Elear

ROGERS, Finella H. 25 Oct 1827 – 20 Dec 1887 sister

ROHR, Susan Jane 1833 – 1921

ROW, Eliza W. 12 Oct 1831 – 25 Oct 1895 wife of John S.
    John S. 24 Jan 1831 – 10 Apr 1892 husb of Eliza W.

ROWE, E.W. [Dr.] 10 Nov 1836 – 23 May 1900 husb of Ida L.
    Ida L. 19 Nov 1848 – 24 Aug 1882 wife of Dr. E.W. Rowe
    Mary Elinor 9 Feb 1878 – a Aug 1878 dau of Dr. E.W. and Ida L. Rowe
    Thomas E. 30 July 1876 – 11 Sept 1877 son of Dr E.W. and Ida L. Rowe

SALE, Laura Jane ... see DUNN
    Mary Elizabeth ,,, see GRASTY
    Mary Spotswood 1851 – 1916 wife of William D. Sale, in Hull plot
    Virginia Margaret ... see MOORE
    William Davis 1848 – 1916 husb of Mary S., in Hull plot

SANFORD, Lelia Johnson 26 Nov 1890 – 3 Feb 1869

SCOTT, Susan Catherine Graves 25 Nov 1841 – 29 Mar 1918 wife of James Martin
                Scott in Coleman plot

SEAL, John W. 12 Nov 1824 – 20 Feb 1909 husb of Louansy
    Louansy 3 Mar 1822 – 29 June 1889 wife of John W.

SELBY, Benjamin F. sr 14 Sept 1848 – 7 Feb 1934 husb of Lydia Gosnell, farmer
    Lydia Gosnell 28 Oct 1853 – 4 Aug 1944 wife of Benjamin F. sr.

SHAW, Fannie Stanard 1835 – 1907 wife of Thomas J.
    Thomas J. 6 Nov 1819 – 18 Sept 1894 husb of Fannie S., born in Prince
                William County, Virginia

SHEPHERD, James 17 June 1790 – 21 Aug 1842 near Helen Elear and James Robin-
                son

SIMS, Lucy A. 1849 - 1933 mother, wife of Wilson T.Sims
    Wilson T. 1847 - 1943 father, husb of Lucy A.

SLAUGHTER, Eugenia Taylor 1842 - 1929 wife of Dr. Alfred E. Slaughter

SMITH, Mary H. 1839 - 1929
    Mary Hansbrough b & d 10 Mar 1894
    Morris Chabels d. 17 Apr 1888 42nd year
    W. J. 1 Oct 1832 - 20 Dec 1908
    William J. 1842 - 1928

SPARKS, Nannie Harrison 25 Oct 1844 - 20 Apr 1916 wife of Robert W.
    Robert W. 3 June 1840 - 4 Oct 1902

SPOTSWOOD, Mary ... see SALE

STANARD, Fannie ... see SHAW
    Mary ... see CHAPMAN

STEPHENS, Joseph H. 10 Aug 1834 - 20 Jan 1871 husb of Martha
    Martha 22 Mar 1837 - 25 Mar 1875 wife of Joseph H.

STOVIN, Bettie B. Newman 28 May 1840 - 12 June 1892 wife of Charles J.
    Charles J. sr 12 Aug 1809 - 20 Feb 1895
    Charles James 1868 - 1912
    Maude Taylor 1 Sept 1866 - 22 Nov 1898 wife of Charles J. jr

STRICKLER, Harrison 25 Jan 1848 - 26 Oct 1924 father, husb of Sarah J.
    Sarah J. 7 June 1854 - 29 Feb 1928   wife of Harrison

TALIAFERRO, Anthony Barclay 23 Oct 1884 - 20 Feb 1957 husb of Kathleen N.
    Charlotte Franklin 12 Nov 1854 - 20 Nov 1894 born in Delaware, died at
                    "Annandale, Rapidan, Orange County, Virginia, dau
                    of Rev. and Mrs. Ben Franklin
    Edmund Pendleton 8 Oct 1849 - 15 Aug 1927
    Edmund Pendleton [Dr.] 15 Nov 1809 - 7 Jan 1886 husb of Octavia H.
    Eleanor ... see NELSON
    Harriet Bynam Tinsley 18 Sept 1829 - 5 Mar 1903 wife of Jaquelin
    Jaquelin P. 17 Mar 1817 - 10 Apr 1889 husb of Harriet B. T.
    John [Capt.] 1843 - 1917 with Anthony B. and Kathleen
    Kathleen Newman 28 Aug 1889-   wife of Anthony B.
    Lucy Willis ... see BRADLEY
    Mary Wilkinson 21 Apr 1844 - 5 June 1913 wife of C.C. Taliaferro
    Octavia Hortense 17 Nov 1818 - 13 Jan 1897 wife of Dr. E.P. Taliaferro
    Thomas Garland 15 Oct 1849 - 25 Sept 1930
    Victoria T. ... see WALLACE
    William Alexander 13 Oct 1851 - 6 May 1926 born in Gloucester County,
                    Virginia, died at "Annandale, Rapidan, Virginia son
                    of Brig. Genl. and Mrs Alexander Galt Taliaferro, CSA

TATUM, Lucy ... see BOND

TAYLOR, Anna W.L. ... see BURGESS
    Edmund Pendleton 27 Sept 1854 - 23 Sept 1911, eldest son of Erasmus and
                    Roberta A. Taylor
    Maud ... see STOVIN

TENNANT, David B. no dates husb of Mary W.
    Mary W. 18 Oct 1832 - 28 Sept 1852 wife of David B., born in Madison Coun-
                    ty, Virginia, died in New York

TERRILL, Florence Dickenson 1860 - 1929 wife of Wm E.T. Terrill
    Janett [Mrs.] 21 Sept 1795 - 2 Feb 1870
    Susan M. 11 June 1829 - 10 Feb 1897 wife of Towles Terrill "Little Sister"

TERRILL, Robert M. [Dr.] 22 Dec 1838 – 5 Feb 1870
    Towles 20 Mar 1831 – 30 Oct 1916 husb of Susan M., Member Montpelier
                 Guards Stonewall Brigade CSA
    Uriel [Dr.] 9 Apr 1793 – 3 July 1885
    William Edward Thomas 1843 – 1914

TIGNOR, Florida Farrar 27 Dec 1865 – 7 Oct 1948 wife of Thomas J.
    Mildred 1 Nov 1896 – 7 June 1897 dau of T.J. and F.F. Tignor
    Thomas J. 19 Jan 1863 – 3 Aug 1929

TINSLEY, Harriet Bynam ... see TALIAFERRO

TUEL, Isaac 26 Jan 1833 – 11 Feb 1919 erected by his son, J.P.

WALKER, Anne Carter 1848 – 1928 with Robert S.
    Eliza S. 3 Dec 1827 – 22 Jan 1829
    Eloise Rice ... see HALSEY
    John S. 14 July 1809 – 18 Feb 1893 "In memory of my father"
    Joseph 28 June 1836 – 22 Oct 1862
    Robert Stringfellow 1840 – 1914
    Sallie 27 July 1834 – 19 Jan 1899
    Susan H. 11 Apr 1809 – 22 Sept 1867

WALLACE, Victoria T. d. 25 July 1892 wife of Thomas P. Wallace, dau of
                Dr. E.P. and O.H. Taliaferro

WAMBERSIE, Alice Parker 14 Jan 1858 – 7 Feb 1932 wife of Capt. John E.
    John Edward [Capt.] 17 June 1836 – 11 June 1919 husb of Alice P.

WARNER, Helen M. 21 Aug 1804 – 3 July 1834
    Mary ... see BANKHEAD

WARREN, Alice Hurkamp 25 Nov 1852 – 29 Jan 1941 wife of Henry I. (probably
                "Harry" since she was beside Harry and no Henry
                was found)
    Harry Innes [Capt] 7 Apr 1847 – 25 Oct 1920 CSA

WATERMAN, Mary ... see GRAHAM

WATSON, Joab L. 20 Oct 1845 – 27 Jan 1917 husb of Mary F.
    Mary Francis May 1846 – 1938 wife of Joab L.

WATTLES, Andrew Jackson 16 Sept 1843 – 9 July 1926 husb of Mary Eliza
    Mary Eliza 23 Nov 1849 – 14 Jan 1927 wife of Andrew J.

WEBB, Effie 1882 – 1965 dau of Harriet E. same stone with Harriet E.
    Harriet Elizabeth 1842 – 1927 mother of Effie on same stone

WELCH, Wilhelmina G. ... see GRAVES

WHITLOCK, Bettie S. 19 Aug 1834 – 14 June 1913
    Byrd Lee 22 July 1861 – 1878
    George [W?] 26 Nov 1834 – 2 May 1904
    Martha M. 29 May 1830 – 1 Feb 1888 sister

WILHOIT, Jacob N. 26 Sept 1867 – 20 Mar 1898
    John Newton 1839 – 1926 husb of Sarah E.
    Sarah Elizabeth 1841 – 1936 wife of John N.

WILKINSON, Mary ... see TALIAFERRO

WILLEROY, Matilda ... see DANIEL

WILLIAMS, Emily Brent no dates inf dau of Wm G. and R.B. Williams

WILLIAMS, Evelyn Johnson 20 Jan 1859 - 1 Nov 1931 wife of William C. Williams
    Evelyn K. 16 Oct 1890 - 27 June 1892 dau of Wm and Evelyn Williams
    Hubert no dates inf son of Wm G. and R.B. Williams
    Mildred Pendleton ... see BOOTON
    Richard Catlett 17 June 1862 - 2 Apr 1888
    Roberta Banks 13 Dec 1838 - 18 Jan 1906 wife of Wm G. Williams
    William Clayton jr 13 May 1884 - 2 Nov 1945
    William Grymes 8 Nov 1829 - 17 Dec 1901

WILLIS, H.L. 1846 - 1922 CSA in Eckloff lot
    Lewis d. 9 Sept 1852 age 24 years
    Lucy Mary (Nee Nalle) d. 15 Dec 1855 age 45 years wife of B.D. Willis
    Lucy T. 12 May 1846 - 21 Oct 1880
    Nellie Conway 1 Oct 1848 - 7 May 1923 with William B.Willis
    Richard H. June 1801 - Apr 1885
    Richard Henry 12 Aug 1849 - 1 Jan 1900
    William Byrd 23 Mar 1836 - 18 Aug 1913

WILTSHIRE, Joseph A. 14 July 1849 - 11 Aug 1927 husb of Sarah E.
    Sarah Elizabeth 29 Dec 1852 - 26 Apr 1930 wife of Jos A.
    W. B. 23 Jan 1836 - 5 Mar 1911 son of J.A. and S.E. Wiltshire

WINN, Mary J. 1840 - 1897
    Thomas J. 1838 - 1910

WINSLOW, Frederick W. d. 21 Dec 1896 77th year husb of Martha J.
    Martha J. d. 1 Mar 1907 84th year wife of F.W.

WOODRIFF, Florence Jaffray 28 Feb 1851 - 3 Jan 1930 born in N.Y. wife of
                                                        John R.P.Woodriff
    John R.P. 14 May 1850 - 9 Oct 1929 born in Malcombe Regis, Dorsetshire

WRIGHT, Lucy C. 18 May 1841 - 24 July 1902 wife of W. Andrew
    W. Andrew 12 June 1844 - 27 July 1910 husb of Lucy C.

YAGER, Champ Conner 7 Dec 1834 - 11 Sept 1902
    Sallie W. 5 June 1846 - 11 June 1914

YANCEY, Jane E. 23 Sept 1816 - 27 July 1888
    Janett 12 July 1855 - 28 June 1856
    Jno. W. 7 Mar 1803 - 3 Aug 1894
    Sarah M. T. d. 20 Apr 1849

YATES, George N. 5 Sept 1857 - 21 Mar 1881 son of Snowden and Margaret P.
    Margaret P. d. 20 Dec 1887 wife of Snowden Yates

YOUNG, Charles O. d. 2 Mar 1862 26 years

LEWISTOWN CEMETERY

DIRECTIONS: Route 20 West to Route 611 North to Route 603
             Northeast for 1.8 miles. Cemetery is in triangle
             formed by fork of Route 603 and Route 715

Earliest birthdate: 1865
Earliest death date: 1921
Total number of tombstones: 44 plus many, many unmarked graves

MAPLEWOOD CEMETERY

DIRECTIONS: From Gordonsville, Virginia West on Route 33
              for 0.5 miles. Cemetery is on right at the
              edge of town.

MONUMENT TO CIVIL WAR SOLDIERS "Maplewood Memorial Association has
              erected this tablet as a tribute of respect to some
              700 confederate soldiers, mainly from N.C. and Ga.
              who laid down their lives for the cause they loved and
              lost. Their names are perished may their memory be
              imperishable!"

ACREE, John Thomas 23 Sept 1850 - 31 Dec 1913

ALLAN, David W. no dates Co I 11 Va Inf CSA
      Maria Louise ... see FAULCONER

ALLMAN, Mary 1898 infant
      Mary Denton 20 Dec 1834 - 18 Nov 1901 mother
      Ralph L. 1896 infant

ATKINS, Benjamine F. 25 July 1850 - 13 Apr 1943 husb of Mildred E.
      Mildred E. Newman ... see NEWMAN
      S.C. d. 10 Mar 1891 age 65 years 11 months 12 days wife of Samuel G.
      Samuel G. d. 24 Dec 1879 age 52 years 6 months 27 days husb of S.C.

BAILES, Merritt d. 27 Mar 1887 age 45 in Seth Conner Brown plot

BAILEY, Charles M. 8 July 1807 - 3 Nov 1878
      Eliz Jane 27 Jan 1833 - 10 May 1909
      James Thomas 16 Sept 1840 - 29 July 1911 Lt. Conf. Vet. husb of Lavenia H.
      John C. no dates Co H 57 Va Inf CSA
      John Coleman 19 Nov 1876 - 27 Oct 1878 son of J.T. and Luvenia H. Bailey
      Lavenia Harriet Gilbert 23 July 1854 - 26 Dec 1936 wife of James T.
      Nancy Frances 3 Aug 1835 - 10 Sept 1914

BAKER, Elizabeth Moore d. 27 July 1884
      Frances E. Mahanes 10 Sept 1850 - 19 Feb 1920 wife of Wm. Martin Baker

BARBOUR, Jennie F. d. 20 Jan 1917 beside Philip P in Somerville-Barbour plot
      Philip Pendleton 23 Oct 1839 - 26 Jan 1914 CSA beside Jennie F. in
                        Somerville - Barbour plot

BAUGHAM, Bettie Shepherd 30 Mar 1848 - 1 May 1931 wife of Richard A.
      Henry Peyton 8 Sept 1872 - 26 Nov 1933 with Richard Linwood Baugham
      Richard Alexander 9 Jan 1828 - 4 Oct 1900 husb of Bettie S.
      Richard Linwood 5 Apr 1886 - 23 Sept 1887 with Henry P.

BAUGHAN, Susie May ... see GOODWIN

BAUSMAN, Sarah ... see McELROY

BEALE, Charles 3 Oct 1795 - 23 Apr 1853 husb of Clementine V. one weathered
                        stone with five names: Charles, Charles L. Clementine,
                        James Goss, and Wm Herbert Beale. Charles listed as
                        Dr.
      Charles L. 9 Apr 1851 - 14 Feb 1889 see above

BEALE, Clementine V. 8 Aug 1825 - 19 Nov 1885 wife of Dr. Charles W. Beale
                    see note with Dr. Charles
    James Goss 31 Jan 1865 - 25 Sept 1910 see note with Charles
    James Newton 20 Apr 1840 - 25 Mar 1865
    Mary.H. 1 May 1791 - 24 Mar 1882 Our Mother
    Wm Herbert 8 Feb 1859 - 12 July 1884 see note with Charles

BECK, Reuben 25 Apr 1818 - 19 July 1896

BERKELEY, Wm Scott 19 Aug 1838 - 21 May 1889

BICKERS, Julia M. 4 July 1833 - 26 July 1902 wife of J.B.Morris in J. Harlow
    plot

BISPHAM, James Skinker 20 May 1853 - 29 July 1930 husb of Mattie Adelaid
    Mattie Adelaid b. Sept 1848   wife of James Skinker Bispham

BLEDSOE, Lou Willie 4 May 1898 - 25 May 1898
    Mildred H. ... see PROCTOR

BOSTON, Evdora B. 28 Oct 1848 - 17 Dec 1918 wife of Henry L.
    Henry L. 19 Feb 1851 - 18 Mar 1900 husb of Evdora B.

BOUGHAN, Annie E. 23 Jan 1838 - 11 Oct 1920
    John Claude 1 Jan 1868 - 14 Nov 1890
    Lutie Blanch 3 Oct 1869 - 24 Nov 1891
    Nathaniel James d. 19 Jan 1890 age 97 years 2 months 27 days   CSA

BOWEN, Ella May ... see KEYSER
    Emmett Wilbur 16 Aug 1972 - 14 Jan 1945 husb of Fannie Etchison
    Fannie Etchison 13 Mar 1876 - 17 Feb 1915 wife of Emmett W.
    Infant b & d 21 Sept 1895 dau of Emmett W. and Fannie E. Bowen
    L.D. 2 Jan 1826 - 23 Jan 1893
    S.F. d. 18 June 1913 age 68 years

BRAGG, Ada H. 10 Feb 1858 - 16 May 1905 wife of J.R.
    Cornelia Frances 3 Apr 1842 - 14 Feb 1879
    Elizabeth 1833 - 1898
    James R. 18 Mar 1813 - 8 Apr 1892
    James R. 29 July 1847 - 26 Sept 1901 husb of Ada H.
    John G. 1887 - 1889
    Julia A. 1815 - 1902
    Mary E. 1836 - 1883
    Maurice J. 1869 - 1888
    Sallie F. 1842 - 1894
    Virgil Thomas 16 Oct 1841 - 8 Aug 1923
    William B. 1849 - 1900

BRENT, Bessie Seymour 1846 - 1924

BRISCO, Fleming 20 Apr 1845 - 17 Mar 1901 3rd son of Robert Brisco of Crofton
                Hall, Wiglon, England

BROWN, Jennie Elizabeth 1851 - 1887
    Seth Conner 1832 - 1886
    Wm Neil d. 24 Mar 1878 age 9 years

BRUCE, Annie Elisebeth 10 Sept 1848 - 18 Oct 1907 wife of R.L.Bruce
    Hamilton L. 15 July 1872 - 14 Feb 1898 husb of Mamie A.
    L.W. 22 Oct 1856 - 8 Oct 1890 my husband
    Mary Alice 19 Apr 1850 - 9 Dec 1920 wife of Richard
    Richard d. 6 Apr 1903 father, husb of Mary Alice

BUCKLEY, Margaret d. 30 Aug 1894 56 years native of County Clare, Ireland

BUDDECKE, Christian Theodore 9 Nov 1809 – 6 Mar 1891 husb of Julia W.M.
    Julia Wilson Marriner 4 June 1820 – 20 June 1876 wife of Christian T.

BURNAM, Alice [Miss.] Apr 1851 – Nov 1920 [also spelled BURNHAM]
    Laura [Miss.] Mar 1845 – Feb 1922
    Mary E. 18 Aug 1811 – 31 Jan 1834 our mother

BUTLER, A.C. 20 Mar 1837 – 28 Nov 1897 "Our Dear Daughter"
    M. Alice d. 8 Mar 1888 22 years wife of M.A.Butler
    Mary A. [Mrs.] 22 June 1825 – 10 Oct 1901 Our Mother

CARTER, M.A. ... see DETTOR

(?CLARK or ?FABER), Minnie Lillian d. 4 May 1897 daughter, broken stone in
                Clark-Faber plot

CLARKSON, Laura J. 4 Oct 1821 – 3 Nov 1904
    Nancy M. 24 Feb 1787 – 15 Sept 1824

CHAMBERS, Mary ... see PORTER

CLOWES, Amos K. 15 Dec 1838 – 25 May 1919 husb of Helen V.
    Helen V. 21 Jan 1843 – 31 Oct 1921 wife of Amos K.

COATES, Margaret H. 1832 – 1904

COLLINS, Ann M. 21 Jan 1856 – 17 Dec 1925 mother, 2nd wife of James S. Collins
    Eleanor Davis 1872 – 1876 dau of J.S. and L.D. Collins
    James Samuel 20 Sept 1839 – 13 June 1923 father, husb of 1] Lucy D. and
                2] Ann M.
    Lucy D. 1 Apr 1846 – 31 July 1882 1st wife of James S. Collins

COLVIN, W. C. 2 May 1833 – 25 Feb 1895

CONLEY, Angeline d. 22 Dec 1945 110 years

CONWAY, Maggie G. 1 Sept 1840 – 10 Apr 1883 wife of Frank C. Fitzhugh

COWHERD, Adeline R. Harris 1847 – 1941 wife of Marcellus D. Cowherd
    Ernest H. 21 Apr 1880 – 7 Nov 1890 son of M.D. and A.R. Cowherd
    Marcellus D. no dates. husb of Adeline R. Harris, Sgt Co C 13 Va Inf CSA
    Mary L. 29 Aug 1872 – 14 Oct 1893 dau of M.D. and A.R. Cowherd
    Norine Victoria 1898 – 1900
    Susan L. 11 Oct 1829 – 5 Apr 1880 wife of E.F. Cowherd

COX, Minnie L. 10 May 1874 – 4 Sept 1895 wife of W.P.Stuntz, in Bailey plot

CREEL, Arabella McMullan 4 Dec 1856 – 17 May 1946 beside Benjamin
    Benjamin F. 30 Aug 1837 – 3 July 1916 beside Arabella

CRISP, Pamela d. 1 Oct 1873 age 60 years died in Gordonsville, Virginia
                in Dunn lot

CURTISS, Dollie 12 June 1892 – 16 June 1892 dau of O.B. and G.G. Curtiss
    Emma 19 Aug 1886 – 4 Aug 1887 dau of O.B. and G.G. Curtiss

DANDRIDGE, Mary V. 1842 – 1921 wife of William B.
    William B. 1852 – 1919 husb of Mary V.

DANIEL, Cornelia 4 Apr 1837 – 9 Aug 1903 age 66 years
    Sarah Travers 1856 – 1945 wife of Henry Clay Eddins

DAVENPORT, Ann ... see HOOKER
    John T. 26 June 1831 – 27 Oct 1902

DAVENPORT, John T. 16 Jan 1836 - 20 Dec 1905

DAVIS, A.A. [Dr.] 5 July 1827 - Apr 1860
    Elizabeth W. 20 July 1811 - 22 Oct 1884
    John W. 3 Apr 1849 - 29 Apr 1904 husb of May Phillips
    May Phillips 23 Dec 1854 - 18 June 1909 wife of John W.
    Sarah 14 Nov 1791 - 17 July 1880 wife of W.T.
    Sarah A. 24 Aug 1823 - 23 Sept 1896
    William Dudley 27 July 1836 - Sept 1867
    William J. 8 Jan 1809 - 10 Oct 1875
    William T. 5 Nov 1785 - 27 July 1858 husb of Sarah

DENTON, Mary ... see ALLMAN

DETTOR, Lillian A. ... see DOWELL
    M. A. 20 Jan 1845 - 23 Nov 1938 wife of W.F., dau of W.S. and M.A. Carter
    W.F. 9 Aug 1840 - 6 Apr 1911 husb of M. A., son of Jos and Margaret Dettor

DICKINSON, Jane ... see MARTIN

DODD, Sarah ... see REYNOLDS

DOLIN, Elizabeth M. Stuckdell ,,, see STUCKDELL
    Johnnie R. 8 Jan 1859 - 8 Oct 1886 son of Thomas and Elizabeth Dolin,
                        killed by a side bridge near Carlisle, Ky. while dis-
                        charging his duty as conductor on the KCRR
    Thomas 2 Apr 1827 - 15 Nov 1904 husb of Elizabeth M.S.

DOUGLESS, Henry 6 Dec 1849 - 20 Mar 1937

DOVEL, E. G. 1874 - 1875
    E.S. 1869 - 1869
    George D. 6 Aug 1843 - 30 Mar 1905 husb of Mary J., our father
    J. C. 1880 - 1880
    L. W. 1870 - 1870
    Mary J. 11 Aug 1845 - 28 Sept 1918 wife of George D., our mother

DOWELL, Berryman 1806 - Jan 1897 husb of Margaret
    J. M. 31 Jan 1850 - 31 Jan 1921
    Lemuel 6 Mar 1838 - 28 July 1906 husb of Marietta
    Lillian A. 23 Oct 1867 - 16 Mar 1887 wife of Wm L. Dowell, dau of William F.
                        and M.A. Dettor
    Lutie J. 15 June 1896 - 19 May 1897
    Margaret 1808 - 1898 age 91 wife of Berryman Dowell
    Marietta 31 Oct 1840 - 31 May 1911 wife of Lemuel
    Susan Catherine 15 Feb 1847 - 14 Mar 1917 wife of Tazewell F.
    Tazewell Franklin 18 Sept 1846 - 18 Apr 1918 husb of Susan C.

DOWNER, Carrie Maude 2 Feb 1891 - 26 Mar 1892 dau of W.R. and Willie M. Downer
    Lucy M. 28 Aug 1832 - 13 June 1907
    Mollie 22 Feb 1861 - 9 Jan 1916 wife of James S. Watkins sr, mother of
                        James S. Watkins jr
    W. W. 7 Oct 1832 - 9 Jan 1921 father
    William R. 19 May 1857 - 24 June 1911 husb of Willie M.
    Willie McMullan 6 Mar 1864 - 13 Oct 1951

DUNN, Ada ... see ROGERS
    B. F. [Dr.] d. 7 Mar 1885 age 64 years, husband
    Cora d. 26 June 1863 age 18 months
    F.W. [Lt.] d. 16 Mar 1898 age 29 years in Cuba US Vol Signal Corps
    Ida d. 22 Aug 1864 age 5 years and 7 months
    Maria d. 25 Nov 1865 age 18 months
    Mary S. 13 July 1830 - 13 Feb 1911 wife of Wm M. Dunn
    Scott d. 2 Oct 1869 age 12 months

DUNN, William M. 28 June 1823 - 15 May 1891 Mason, husb of Mary S.

EARLY, Ida Kingman ... see THORNTON

EDDINS, Charlotte J. ... see GOODLOE
    Henry Clay 1844 - 1912 husb of Sarah Travers Daniel
    Richard Oscar 1848 - 1934 father, husb of Sarah Ellen Marshall
    Sarah Ellen Marshall 1849 - 1928 wife of Richard O.
    Sarah Travers Daniel ... see DANIEL

EGGLESTON, Elnora Virginia d. 3 June 1916 69 years wife of R. I Eggleston

ELENDER, Mattie ... see MARTIN

ELLIOTT, Mary A. d. 15 Nov 1916 age 90 years in Dunn lot

ELLIS, Clara ... see SNEED

ESTES, Blanche Talley 1861 - 1893

ETCHISON, Fannie ... see BOWEN

EUBANK, George F. 16 Mar 1884 - 17 Jan 1885 (two blank spaces)

EVANS, Annie Norvill 7 Dec 1816 - 8 Aug 1867 mother, wife of James A.
    James A. 11 Sept 1814 - 29 Feb 1888 father, husb of Annie N.
    Virginia Taylor 13 Dec 1846 - 12 Feb 1896 wife of H.B. Linney

FABER, Ann M. 16 Dec 1828 - 19 May 1891 wife of John G.
    Annie Belle 23 Apr 1880 - 30 June 1880 dau of L.J. and M.L. Faber
    Bettie J. 22 Oct 1847 - 8 Jan 1913
    John G. no dates Co D 19 Va Inf CSA husb of Ann M.
    John W. d. 14 Mar 1877 inf son of L.J. and M.L. Faber
    Lewis Joel 11 Oct 1856 - 1 June 1934 father, husb of Mary Lucy
    Mary Lucy Jordan 28 June 1858 - 20 Sept 1927 mother, wife of Lewis J.
    Minnie Lillian ... see CLARK
    Sallie A. 21 Apr 1861 - 18 Oct 1892 wife of Charles H. Marshall

FAULCONER, Edward Jackson 1828 - 1883 husb of Maria Louise Allan
    Maria Louise Allan 1828 - 1910 wife of Edw J.

FITZHUGH, Francis Conway 12 Aug 1838 - 12 May 1910 husb of Maggie G. Conway
    Maggie G. Conway ... see CONWAY

FLEWELLEN, Majjp 1 May 1828 - 19 Apr 1910

FRENCH, James Strange 1808 - 1886
    Laura ... see HUTT
    Laura George 1832 - 1907

GARRISON, Ann 15 Feb 1813 - 9 Feb 1902 wife of R.Q.Garrison
    Sarah E. 19 May 1833 - 9 Nov 1917

GAY, L. [Mrs.] 1 Feb 1849 - 20 June 1897

GENTRY, S. J. 17 July 1863 - 21 Dec 1900 husb of Lottie Lee
    Sarah [Mrs.] 22 Mar 1797 - 1 Aug 1875 grandmother with Susie A. Jordan

GEORGE, Laura ... see FRENCH

GILBERT, Lavenia Harriet ... see BAILEY

GOOCH, Helen ... see SMITHERS

GOODLOE, Charlotte J. Eddins 1853 - 1928 wife of Spotswood H. Goodloe
    John Robert d. 27 Nov 1887 age 10 years 4 months son of J.G. and E.M.
        Goodloe
    Spotswood H. 1833 - 1913 Mason, husb of Charlotte J. Eddins

GOODWIN, Harry Wallace 17 Jan 1895 - 26 May 1895 son of P. M. and S.M.
        Goodwin
    Lucy A. 28 Nov 1857 - 19 Jan 1875
    Mary A. d. 27 Jan 1867 age 63 years wife of John Goodwin
    Mary E. 21 Feb 1877 - 15 Nov 1890
    Nannie A. 3 Dec 1835 - 2 Mar 1913 wife of Andrew J. Lynn in Slaughter
            plot
    P. Marvin 18 Apr 1861 - 10 Mar 1938 husb of Susie May Baughan
    Susie May Baughan 29 Oct 1870 - 3 Feb 1918 wife of P.M. Goodwin

GORDON, James 22 July 1787 - 13 June 1825
    Lucy ... see LINNEY

GRAVES, C. Eudora ... see SCOTT

GREINER, Christopher C. 1841 - 1923 husb of Roberta J. Watts
    Roberta J. Watts 1854 - 1925 wife of Christopher C.

HALL, Jane L. 16 May 1844 - 12 Feb 1929 grandmother
    Joseph Hastin 26 Apr 1859 - 7 Jan 1919 husb of Sallie Walton Hall
    Livie W. 3 Mar 1900 - 19 July 1900
    Nannie A. 4 Feb 1855 - 4 Sept 1891
    Sallie Walton 4 Nov 1861 - 26 Mar 1939 wife of Joseph H., "Our Mother"
    Walton 25 Oct 1886 - 19 June 1889 son of J.H. and S.W. Hall

HARLOW, John W. 30 Dec 1844 - 16 Jan 1921 husb of Zulemma H. Morris
    Zulemma H. Morris ... see MORRIS

HARRIS, Adeline R. ... see COWHERD
    Lucy M. 1838 - 1890 wife of Richard H.
    Richard H. 1837 - 1920 husb of Lucy M., father

HARRISON, Cassius A. 7 Oct 1850 - 17 Apr 1899
    Clara G. 31 Jan 1846 - 26 Apr 1914 mother, wife of George F.
    George Fisher 9 Apr 1846 - 17 Jan 1925 CSA, husb Clara G.

HART, Elizabeth H. 1870 - 1957 beside Thomas W.
    Thomas W. 1847 - 1926 beside Elizabeth H.

HEFLIN, Cornelius d. 5 May 1896 age 89 years

HILLS, Thomas Johnson 17 [____] 1839 - 26 July 1861 son of Dennis and Eliza
                    Henderson Hills. Born in Rome Ga., Co G 8th Ga Reg
                    wounded in Battle of Manassas 21 July 1861, removed
                    to Gordonsville, Va. where he died 26 July 1861

HOGAIN, Mary P. [Mrs.] 25 Dec 1845 - 30 Mar 1902 born in Lexington, Va.

HOOKER, Ann Davenport 1807 - 1887

HUCKSTEP, James Edward 6 Jan 1825 - 20 May 1903

HUGHES, Mary Jane 26 June 1821 - 28 Nov 1903 wife of Capt. Lynn B. McMullan

HUGHSON, Elizabeth L. 27 June 1802 - 1 Aug 1884

HUTT, Laura French 1853 - 1892
    William Harvey 1835 - 1894
    William Harvey 1887 - 1889

JEFFERY, Martha L. 30 Mar 1823 - 8 Jan 1896 wife of John W. Walker D.D.

JORDAN, Bettie May 12 Dec 1856 - 13 Oct 1876 wife of W.H. Jordan
   Susie A. [Mrs.] 26 Jan 1834 - 21 Jan 1884 mother, with Mrs Sarah Gentry

KENNON, William 1848 - 1922

KEYS, Charles M. 23 Mar 1841 - 13 Aug 1876 Mason beside Ethel A.
   Ethel A. 12 Dec 1871 - 25 May 1877 beside Charles M.
   Katey d. 4 June 1871 age 16 months dau of S.M. and M.D. Keys

KEYSER, Ella May Bowen 1864 - 1932 wife of Rev. W.H., mother of Oscar L.
   Josephine Elizabeth d. 22 Dec 1900
   Oscar Lee 28 July 1887 - 11 Feb 1889 son of E.M. and W.H. Keyser
   William Hampson [Rev.] 1863 - 1927 husb of Ella May Bowen

KING, Infant d. 14 Sept 1891 child of L.M. and G.A. King

KUBE, William 29 Feb 1832 - 22 Nov 1889

LEAKE, Eva Lena 31 May 1892 - 1 Aug 1892 dau of F.C. and Lena Leake
   F. Carter no dates Carrington's Co Va Lt Arty CSA husb of Lena
   F. M.[Capt] no dates husb of Sarah E. West
   Sarah E. West 18 May 1849 - 30 Dec 1931 wife of Capt F.M. Leake

LINNEY, Charles Beale 1845 - 1935
   Henry Bascom 22 Sept 1847 - 14 Jan 1903 husb of Virginia Taylor Evans
   Henry Marshall [Rev.] 1820 - 1895
   James Harrington 1852 - 1922
   Lucy Gordon 1824 - 1870
   Virginia Taylor Evans ... see EVANS

LOCKER, George 1847 - 1927 husb of Lillian Synan
   Lillian Synan 1860 - 1941 wife of George

LOCKHART, J. E. "Jim" 1865 - 1888
   John A. 1850 - 1901
   Margaret 19 Sept 1852 - 6 June 1882
   Martha M. 7 Oct 1856 - 12 Sept 1872
   Martha Miller 1827 - 1914 born in Ayshire, Scotland, wife of Samuel
   Samuel 1826 - 1900 b. in Ayshire, Scotland, father, husb of Martha Miller
   William M. 16 Mar 1858 - 3 July 1885

LOYD, Cassandra Paxton ... see MANSFIELD

LUSHWAY, Juliet R. 28 Dec 1842 - 5 Sept 1907 wife of Peter
   Peter 22 Apr 1840 - 20 Apr 1932 husb of Juliet R.

LYNN, Andrew J. 8 Sept 1829 - 17 July 1893 husb of Nannie A. Goodwin in
                     Slaughter plot
   Mary Frances 18 May 1843 - 8 Aug 1904 wife of Milton Lynn
   Milton 7 Apr 1837 - 29 Jan 1912 husb of Mary F.
   Nannie A. Goodwin ... see GOODWIN

MAHANES, Emily V. 26 June 1839 - 19 Nov 1905
   Frances E. ... see BAKER
   Samuel Gariet 22 Jan 1855 - 25 Mar 1891 husband
   Tavner O. 31 Dec 1838 - 10 Nov 1904

MANLEY, Annie E. 20 July 1848 - 31 Dec 1898
   G.H. 7 Dec 1844 - 1 Aug 1927 "Our Father"
   James L. 25 Dec 1877 - 5 Jan 1902 son of R.F. and Sallie E. Manley
   Robert F. 11 Oct 1838 - 8 July 1900 same stone as Sallie E. Via and James
                     L. Manley

MANLEY, Sallie E. Via ... see VIA

MANN, Arabella B. 1819 - 3 May 1892 wife of W.H., born in Charlottsville, Va.
                died Alleghany Sta., Va.
    Talbot G. 15 Feb 1849 - 13 Mar 1886 born in Gordonsville, Va., died
                Staunton, Va.
    W.H. 26 Jan 1823 - 13 Mar 1902 husb of Arabella B.

MANSFIELD, Cassandra Paxton 11 May 1807 - 10 Feb 1895 wife of Thos N.
                Mansfield, dau of Thos E. Loyd and Jane Moore Gibson

MARKS, Eliza S. 22 Aug 1865 - 10 Dec 1900

MARRIETT, Angelina M. ... see PATTERSON

MARRINER, Julia Wilson ... see BUDDECKE

MARSH, E. H. 20 Jan 1876 - 23 Jan 1900

MARSHALL, Sallie A. Faber ... see FABER
    Sarah Ellen ... see EDDINS

MARTIN, Jane Dickinson 19 Apr 1850 - 17 Dec 1923 wife of W.H. Martin
    Mary d. 10 May 1889 age 68 years wife of Patrick, "Our Dear Mother"
    Mary 16 Jan 1850 - 4 Aug 1934
    Mattie Elender 19 Aug 1875 - 21 Jan 1898 28 years 5 months and 2 days
    Patrick d. 7 June 1875 70 years husb of Mary, "Our Dear Father"
    William H. 8 July 1842 - 3 May 1919 husb of Jane D. Pvt Va Inf CSA

MASON, Lynea J. ... see SANDERS

MAYHUGH, Coffer 4 Oct 1833 - 25 July 1890 my husband born Dover, Loudon
                County, Virginia, died Gordonsville, Virginia

McALISTE, John T. d. 7 Dec 1901 age 65 years
McALLISTER, Vergie ... see TAYLOR
McELROY, Samuel B. 1827 - 1907
    Sarah Bausman 1832 - 1907

McGEHEE, M. W. 22 Mar 1850 - 19 May 1917 husb of Mary E.
    Mary E. 17 Mar 1846 - 17 Oct 1917· wife of M.W.

McILWAINE, Sammie 8 July 1873 - 6 Dec 1877 son of J.H. and A.G. McIlwaine

McMULLAN, Arabella ... see CREEL
    Mary Jane Hughes ... see HUGHES
    Maude Trevanian 21 Apr 1888 - 24 Aug 1889
    Omer 8 Nov 1896 - 12 Dec 1896
    Virginia ... see MILLER
    Willie ... see DOWNER

McMURRAN, A.S. 19 Sept 1810 - 31 Dec 1890 in HER 81st year
    Charles 7 Nov 1830 - 30 Dec 1893 husb of Jane Peter
    Jane Peter 24 July 1842 - 24 Apr 1905 wife of Charles
    M.V. d. 12 June 1888

MILLER, Martha ... see LOCKHART
    Mary Ellen 1838 - 1926 wife of James Mason Murphy, mother
    Virginia McMullan 1850 - 1931

MITCHELL, Mattie d. 30 Aug 1886 [4?] 0 years

MOORE, Elizabeth ... see BAKER

MORRIS, Hampden Pleasants 1 Apr 1848 – 28 Oct 1907 husb of Zaidee
    Julia M. Bickers ... see BICKERS
    Lemuel no dates Cp F 35 Bn Va Cav CSA
    Zaidee 3 Sept 1859 – 11 Sept 1937 wife of Hampden P.
    Zulemma H. 21 Mar 1856 – 25 Feb 1911 wife of J.W. Harlow

MURPHY, George 20 Mar 1877 – 9 Sept 1878
    H.S. 30 Sept 1869 – 11 Sept 1884
    Mary Ellen Miller ... see MILLER

NEWMAN, Catherine Randolph Taylor 19 Mar 1847 – 30 Dec 1917 wife of Reuben M.
    Conway 29 Apr 1837 – 2 Mar 1917 husb of Eleanor Taylor
    Eleanor 13 Sept 1871 – 17 Oct 1876 dau of Conway and Eleanor Newman
    Eleanor Taylor ... see TAYLOR
    Florence ... see WIRT
    James 1806 – 1866 same stone as Mary S., Sallie J., and J. Sheridan
    J. Sheridan 1880 – 1903 see above
    Mary S. 1804 – 1884 see above
    Mildred E. 26 June 1849 – 17 Apr 1908 wife of B.F. Atkins
    Nannie B. 28 July 1861 – 16 Feb 1903 mother, wife of W.J.Walker
    Nannie Wirt 24 Feb 1848 – 13 Feb 1920 wife of Nathaniel W.
    Nathaniel Welch 27 June 1846 – 3 Oct 1910 husb of Nannie Wirt
    Reuben M. 20 Mar 1843 – 17 Apr 1916 husb of Catherine R.T.
    Sallie J. 1833 – 1909 see James Newman note

NOBLE, Alice V. Riley 27 July 1853 – 6 Jan 1920 wife of John A.
    John A. 4 Mar 1850 – 15 July 1917 husb of Alice V. Riley

NOON, Susie B. ... see TAYLOR

NORVILL, Annie ... see EVANS

OGG, Lydia F. 15 Feb 1835 – 18 June 1907 wife of George W. Runkle

PALMER, Mary Jane 14 Jan 1820 – 17 May 1897 wife of Leonard S. Palmer of
                                Lexington, Virginia

PARROTT, Lucy Jane ... see SMITH

PATTERSON, Angelina M. Marriett 23 Dec 1840 – 30 Oct 1861 dau of I. Patterson
    Willie ... see SNYDER

PAXTON, Cassandra ... see MANSFIELD

PAYNE, Cecil 22 Jan 1876 – 15 Nov 1879
    George A. 28 Aug 1842 – 20 Jan 1890 Mason
    Magnus 20 Aug 1879 – 7 Apr 1881
    Maury 28 May 1882 – 16 Aug 1883

PETER, Jane ... see McMURRAN

PHILLIPS, Camilla C. 26 May 1828 – 4 Sept 1892 wife of Joseph N.
    John Swift 2 Mar 1853 – 18 Mar 1899
    John Wilmer 5 Sept 1890 – 26 June 1892
    Joseph N. 20 Dec 1825 – 31 Mar 1883 husb of Camilla C.
    May ... see DAVIS
    Rosa B. 13 Nov 1849 – 31 July 1910

PORTER, Mary A. M. 1855 – 1875
    Mary Chambers 10 July 1828 – 6 Jan 1901 wife of William Henry married
                        29 Aug 1852 in England
    William Henry 30 Dec 1830 – 22 Feb 1901 husb of Mary Chambers married
                  in England on 29 Aug 1852

PROCTOR, Mildred H. Bledsoe 9 July 1839 - 28 Dec 1888 wife of Orlander
    Orlander 3 Apr 1837 - 31 Dec 1913 husb of Mildred H.

REYNOLDS, Richard Morton 8 May 1847 - 5 Mar 1934 husb of Sarah Dodd
    Sarah Dodd 23 Nov 1849 - 27 Apr 1930 wife of Richard M.

RHODES, George W. 4 Nov 1847 - 23 Apr 1880
    Lilly Mann d. 18 Oct 1882 age 14 months dau of P. and J.L.V. Rhodes

RILEY, Alice V. ... see NOBLE

RINER, Adeline A. d. 3 June 1915 73 years "Aunt Line"

ROBERTSON, J. H. 8 Nov 1840 - 23 July 1903 Mason

ROBINSON, William T. no dates Pollock Co Va Lt Art CSA in Payne lot

ROGERS, Ada Dunn 1866 - 1961 wife of William Samuel
    Infant b & d 20 July 1893 dau of W.S. and A.D. Rogers
    William Samuel 1867 - 1926 husb of Ada Dunn

ROHR, Thomas M. 1849 - 1912

ROUTT, M.E. ... see THURMAN

RUNKLE, George W. 6 Nov 1832 - 30 May 1906 husb of Lydia F. Ogg, Mason
    Lydia F. Ogg ... see OGG

RUSSELL, Sallie T. 3 Apr 1838 - 14 Jan 1919

SANDERS, Lynea J. Mason 3 Mar 1840 - 31 July 1884 wife of John F. Sanders
    William Edward Minor 10 Oct 1866 - 2 Oct 1881 son of J.F. and L.J. Sanders

SARGEANT, H.H.[Dr.] d. 8 June 1910 67 years husb of M.W. Sargeant
    Robert d. 1 Jan 1912 38 years beloved son of Dr. H. H. and M. W.
                                          Sargeant

SCHLOSSER, George William 31 Jan 1846 - 7 Aug 1909 husb of Mary Belle
    Mary Belle 25 Mar 1850 - 23 Aug 1922 wife of George Wm.
    Samuel Gough 1850 - 1907

SCOTT, Anna Pleasants 18 Aug 1853 - 21 May 1928 dau of William C. and Pam-
                                          elia A. Scott
    C. Eudora Graves 1850 - 1930 wife of Edmund Willis Scott
    Charles Lee 6 May 1864 - 8 Mar 1907 son of William C. and Pamelia A. Scott
    Claudia Marshall Willis 18 July 1846 - 23 Jan 1912 married 29 Sept 1869 to
                                          W.W. Scott. "At her left our son, Wyclif"
    Edmund Willis 1852 - 1931 husb of C. Eudora Graves
    Pamelia Augusta 30 Jan 1833 - 8 Dec 1904 wife of Maj. W.C.
    William C. [Maj] Chief Qtrmstr 3rd Arty Corp, Army of Northern Va. CSA
                                          son of John Scott, husb of Pamelia Augusta
    William Wallace 10 Apr 1845 - 16 Jan 1929 husb of Claudia Marshall Willis
                                          A Confederate Soldier Co A (Montpelier Guard 13 Va
                                          Inf) Co H (Black Horse Troop 4th Cav Va)
    Wyclif 27 Dec 1885 - 18 Feb 1906 son of W. W. and Claudia Marshall Scott

SEYMOUR, Bessie ... see BRENT

SHEPHERD, Bettie ... see BAUGHAM

SMITH, A. Custis 6 July 1843 - 7 June 1915
    Edgar Daniel 22 Sept 1881 - 12 Nov 1883 son of Wm J and Lucy J Smith
    Edna M. d. 30 Aug 1890 11 months child of M. M. and M.A. Smith
    George W. 19 Jan 1795 - 3 Feb 1885 grandfather in Dunn lot

SMITH, Lucy Jane Parrott 29 Feb 1844 - 4 Feb 1910 wife of Wm J.
    Sarah A. 1 Nov 1861 - 24 Dec 1896 wife of W. T. jr
    W. T. jr 1 Nov 1861 - 24 Dec 1896 husb of Sarah A. [Note: these dates
                         were double checked and are as they appear on the
                         tombstones]
    William Joseph 21 Sept 1831 - 13 Feb 1887 husb of Lucy Jane Parrott

SMITHERS, C.H. 23 Apr 1857 - 2 Dec 1890
    Helen Gooch 1853 - 1942
    Howard Sale 1835 - 1903
    James Dowell 3 Feb 1876 - 19 Sept 1882 b & d in Gordonsville, Virginia

SNEED, Clara Ellis 12 Feb 1845 - 10 July 1893 wife of John L.
    Elizabeth Woolfolk d. 23 June 1880 age 59 years wife of Littleton W.
    Ellis Hurt 10 Feb 1883 - 11 May 1902 son of John L and Clara E. Sneed
    John Lafayette 12 Jan 1848 - 20 Sept 1905 husb of Clara E.
    John L. 31 May 1877 - 1 June 1926 near Littleton W.
    Littleton Waller d. 27 June 1875 age 62 years husb of Elizabeth W.
    William Henry 4 Dec 1875 - 22 Mar 1897 son of John L. and Clara E. Sneed

SNYDER, Willie 11 May 1818 - 26 Dec 1873 dau of Clementine W. Patterson

SOUDER, Charles M. 5 Nov 1852 - 13 Feb 1892
    Herbert 27 May 1879 - 13 Apr 1885
    L [   ]w 21 Nov 1876 - 2 May 1895

STARRETT, Catherine no dates small stone

STONESIFTER, F.H. 6 Oct 1827 - 6 Oct 1885
    Virginia 8 Feb 1880 - 10 Feb 1880

STRATTON, A. E. d. 27 Jan 1887 age 76 years 1 month and 12 days mother,
                       wife of R. H. Stratton
    George Elmer d. 23 Feb 1881 8 years 5 months and 14 days son of R.H.
                       and M.E. Stratton
    M. E. d. 30 Apr 1897 age 46 years 10 months 13 days wife of Richard H.
    R. H. d. 4 June 1887 age 73 years 1 month 25 days father, husb of A.E.
    Richard Henry 13 Feb 1844 - 29 Sept 1903 husb of M.E. Stratton

STRICKLER, John C. 12 May 1848 - 13 Mar 1918
    Lee K. 7 Nov 1874 - 9 Nov 1898
    Mary J. 12 Mar 1851 - 2 Nov 1898

STUCKDELL, Elizabeth M. 28 Oct 1827 - 30 Dec 1910 wife of Thomas Dolin

STUNTZ, Minnie L. Cox ... see COX

SYNAN, Lillian ... see LOCKER

TALLEY, Blanche ... see ESTES

TATE, _____ b. 90 d. 96 [handcarved, probably 1890 - 1896]
    Addison L. 1844 - 1906 husb of Annie M.
    Alice E. ... see TAYLOR
    Annie M. 1855 - 1907 wife of Addison L. [in separate plot with two unread-
                       able handcarved stones]
    Willie M. 20 Dec 1872 - 15 Apr 1898 son of E.W. and N.E. Gate

TAYLOR, Alice E. 4 Mar 1871 - 19 Jan 1897 wife of W.J. Taylor, dau of N.E.
                      and E.W. Tate
    Allie French 16 Nov 1882 - 16 Dec 1904 brother, son of George W. and
                      Mary Ella Taylor
    Annie Hestell 13 Apr 1893 - 6 June 1909 sister, dau of George W. and Mary
                      Ella Taylor

TAYLOR, Catherine Randolph ... see NEWMAN
   Eleanor 30 Aug 1844 – 8 May 1921 wife of Conway Newman, dau of Robert
      O. and Barbara Taylor
   Elmer C. 29 Dec 1896 – 29 Jan 1897
   George Carter 10 Aug 1887 – 7 June 1906 brother, son of George W. and
      Mary Ella Taylor
   George William 11 Dec 1850 – 10 Mar 1899 father, husb of Mary Ella, father
      of George Carter, Allie French, Ida, William, and
      Annie Hestell
   Hyrum S. 24 Apr 1855 – 29 May 1931 husb of 1] Susie B. Noon and 2]
      Virgie McAllister
   Ida William 12 Mar 1885 – 22 Sept 1893, sister, dau of George W. and
      Mary Ella Taylor
   Mary Ella 1 Mar 1850 – 12 Aug 1914 wife of George W. mother of George
      Carter, Allie French, Ida William, and Annie Hestell
   Susie B. Noon 1857 – 1888 wife of Hyrum S. Taylor
   Virgie McAllister 1870 – 1905 2nd wife of Hyrum S. Taylor

THOMASSON, G. Frank d. 2 Apr 1919 Mason, husb of S.C.
   George Francis 27 Sept 1829 – 25 July 1894 Mason
   Jane O. 5 Nov 1803 – 20 July 1875
   S. C. d. 14 Aug 1904 wife of G.F.

THORNTON, Alice Thurman 6 July 1853 – 2 July 1928 wife of James A.
   Bennie 10 Feb 1889 – 3 July 1889 son of J.A. and A.T. Thornton
   Ida Kingman Early 7 July 1865 – 6 Apr 1931 wife of James A.
   James A. 1870 – 1933 husb of 1] Alice Thurman and 2] Ida Kingman Early

THURMAN, Alice ... see THORNTON
   B. F. d. 4 July 1900 age 69 years husb of M.E. Routt
   M. E. Routt d. 9 Aug 1913 age 87 years wife of B.F.Thurman

TIMBERLAKE, Lucy A. 8 Apr 1835 – 21 Dec 1914 [Note: plot contained following
      footstones that did not appear to match headstones:
      "A.E.M.", "G.J.", "J.F.J.", "M.T.J.", "C.V.J.",
      and "E.S.M."]

TREVANIAN, Maude ... see McMULLAN

TURNER, Virginia Samuel 1861 – 1927 wife of James Henry Wood

TWYMAN, Ettie M. 1 Feb 1866 – 11 Jan 1898

VAUGHAN, Henrietta 1813 – 1890
   Pascall 1803 – 1893

VERLING, George Lee 1872 – 1965 beside Mildred Ann
   Mildred Ann 1835 – 1905 beside George Lee

VIA, Sallie E. 1838 – 1911 wife of R. F. Manley

WALKER, George T. 11 Mar 1871 – 6 June 1896 son of M.A. and H.T. Walker
   Henry T. 21 Aug 1846 – 8 May 1901 husb of M.A.Walker
   H. Wellington 23 Jan 1873 son of H.T. and Millie Walker
   John W.[D.D.] 8 Sept 1819 – 5 Apr 1884 husb of Martha L. Jeffery
   John Weber 10 Mar 1882 – 29 July 1882 son of W.J. and N.B. Walker
   Mildred A. 16 July 1845 – 20 Sept 1907 mother, wife of Henry T. Walker
   Martha L. Jeffery ... see JEFFERY
   Nannie B. Newman ... see NEWMAN
   Walter 13 Nov 1868 – 8 Jan 1872 son of M.A. and H.T. Walker
   William J. 3 Sept 1854 – 10 May 1934 husb of Nannie B. Newman

WALTON, Sallie ... see HALL

WATKINS, James S. sr 10 Dec 1849 – 6 Sept 1935 husb of Mollie Downer, father
                 of James S. jr
    Mollie Downer ... see DOWNER

WATTS, Roberta J. ... see GREINER

WEAVER, B. Franklin 1836 – 1905
    Nellie P. 1847 – 1910

WEBB, Augustine d. 9 Oct 1827 age 65

WEST, Sarah E. ... see LEAKE

WEV, Elizabeth N. 15 Nov 1839 – 4 Jan 1929 mother

WILKINS, George 12 June 1848 – 14 Aug 1928 husb of Lucy E.M.
    Lucy E.M. 7 Nov 1848 – 16 Dec 1934 wife of George

WILLIS, Claudia Marshall ... see SCOTT

WILSON, Julia ... see BUDDECKE

WIRT, Florence Newman 25 Apr 1850 – 11 Jan 1899 wife of Joseph E.
    Joseph E. 8 Mar 1850 – 17 Feb 1889 husb of Florence N.
    Nannie ... see NEWMAN

WOOD, E.M. no dates Co B Cutts G.A. Arty CSA
    James Henry 1849 – 1928 husb of Virginia S. Turner
    Sidney D. 10 Feb 1850 – 23 May 1933 mother
    Virginia Samuel Turner ... see TURNER

WOOLFOLK, Elizabeth ... see SNEED

WORSTER, Arianna d. 11 Jan 1880 in 49th year of her age, wife of M.J. Worster

YAGER, Charles W. 20 Dec 1879 – 3 Aug 1893
    Jos H. 10 Mar 1820 – 31 July 1886
    Sallie D. 20 Mar 1820 – 6 Dec 1890

YOUNG, Cornelia E. 2 June 1850 – 8 Oct 1908 wife of Samuel M. Young
    James S. 28 Mar 1882 – 22 Nov 1882 same stone as Samuel M. and Cornelia
                         E. Young
    Josie S. 19 May 1888 – 7 Aug 1888 same stone as Samuel M. and Cornelia E.
                      Young
    Samuel M. 1852 – 1925 husb of Cornelia E.

YOWELL, James N. 1841 – 1935 Co D 34 Va Inf CSA
    Mary M. 14 May 1841 – 5 Apr 1902 mother

OAKWOOD CEMETERY AT UNIONVILLE

         DIRECTIONS: From intersection of Route 20 and Route 522,
                       take Route 671 to Route 669. Cemetery is on
                       left 0.15 miles after turn.

BOOSE, Eliza ... see SMITH

CLARK, Frank W. 1847 – 1929 CSA husb of Mildred W.
Mildred W. 1850 – 1926 wife of Frank W.

DAWSON, John Carter 1850 – 1937 husb of Lutie Dill
Lutie Dill 1867 – 1931 wife of John Carter Dawson

DILL, Lutie ... see DAWSON

DUNAWAY, Mariette d. 26 Jan 1927 age 87 years mother

McALISTER, Thomas C. 1 Feb 1850 – 5 Dec 1933 husb of Verona L. McAlister
Verona L. 12 Oct 1867 – 6 Dec 1941 wife of Thomas C. McAlister

SMITH, Eliza Boose June 1854 – Jan 1918 wife of James W. Smith
James W. 4 Oct 1846 – 12 Dec 1902 husb of Eliza Boose

WAUGH, Chas A. 24 Sept 1851 – 10 July 1907 husb of Sallie W.
Sallie W. 18 July 1858 – 4 Nov 1896 wife of Charles A.

Total number of tombstones: 207

WESTVIEW CEMETERY

DIRECTIONS: From Orange on Route 20 West 1.5 miles
to cemetery on right. Gate is often
chained and locked. Permission from
house nearby.

CREAL, _____ father, weathered stone beside Dora Creal
Dora 10 Mar 1849 – 12 Aug 1910

DUNCAN, James 18 Sept 1857 – 15 Oct 1889 son of William and Amelia Duncan
William 1831 – 1904 73 years and 10 months

EAST, Willie died ____ [rest of stone crumbled]

JONES, Maggie 20 June 1876 – 22 Feb 1893

McDANIEL, Madison 1840 – 14 May 1913

PIERCE, Patsey 27 July 1867 – 16 Apr 1891

REID, Albert 3 Feb 1839 – 9 Jan 1913
Eugenia 31 Dec 1887 – 22 May 1891

TAYLOR, Charles 1841 – 1919 beside Rebecca
Rebecca 1853 – 1919 mother, wife of Charles W.

WALKER, Pollie B. 30 Dec 1865 – 11 May 1891 wife of T.G.Walker

WHARTON, Charlotte A. d. 10 Jan 1913 age 80 years, mother, beside
Jefferson Wharton
Jefferson d. 24 Oct 1911 age 86 years, father, beside Charlotte
A. Wharton

WOODBERRY CEMETERY AT GORDONSVILLE

DIRECTIONS: From Preddy's Funeral Home on Route 15/33 go
East on T1012 to T1024 then take next road to
right past several burned out houses and a
trailer to Route 710. Cemetery is at end of
road which circles through it.

COLSTON, Celia d. 14 Jan 1907 age 60 years same stone as Martha West and
Rev. D. Parker

GILES, Agnes d. 9 Nov 1885 age 89 years

GORDEN, Sarah 14 Dec 1881 - 8 Dec 1901

McCALL, C. Cadoza 18 Feb 1892 - 4 Jan 1897

PARKER, D.[Rev.] d. 30 July 1900 age 69 years same stone as Martha West and
Celia Colston

REED, Mille 1 June 1835 - 23 Dec 1915 80 years

ROBINSON, Charlotte H. 3 Apr 1862 - 8 Dec 1890
George 18 June 1831 - 15 Aug 1891 beside Mary J.
Mary J. d. 19 Mar 1911 in her 82nd year beside George

THOMAS, Henry d. 24 Feb 1910 age 76 years

VAUGHAN, T. W. [Rev.] d. 12 Mar 1900 age 45 years my beloved husband

WEST, Martha d. 17 Sept 1892 same stone as Celia Colston and Rev. D. Parker

WILLIAMS, Wesley 1846 - 1906

Total number of tombstones: 110 plus many many unmarked and sunken graves.
Much of this cemetery is so overgrown that it was
difficult to find all of the stones that may have
been in the cemetery.

CHURCH CEMETERIES
* * *

ANTIOCH BAPTIST CHURCH CEMETERY

DIRECTIONS: West on Route 20 to South on Route 621 for
1.68 miles to right on Route 692 for 1.6 miles
to church and cemetery on right.

BISCOE, A. W. 24 Oct 1859 - 27 Feb 1919
    Lulu Jane 5 Sept 1892 - 7 Dec 1894 dau of S.W. and A.W. Biscoe
    Susan R. 20 Jan 1825 - 4 Oct 1908
    Susie Wright ... see WRIGHT
    William [Capt.] 27 Sept 1813 - 29 July 1904

BURR, Mollie E. 11 Feb 1843 - 23 Jan 1918

CANADY, Alice R. 16 Sept 1849 - 14 July 1926 wife of John Arthur Webb

CHILDRESS, Lydia J. 21 June 1845 - 23 June 1904 wife of William E. Childress
    William E. July 1842 - 28 Nov 1909 husb of Lydia J.

CLARKE, Robert L. 20 Nov 1846 - 7 Oct 1936
    Susan R. 8 Feb 1843 - 28 Aug 1910

COLEMAN, Frazier no dates Co I 6 Va Cav CSA
    Mary A. 19 May 1842 - 9 May 1892

COOPER, Beverly S. 3 Aug 1849 - 23 Nov 1925 same stone as Roberta C.
    Roberta C. 1 July 1865 - 7 Nov 1934 same stone as Beverly S.

DEWEY, Annie ... see SMITH

GARDNER, Alexander d. April 1912 age 64 years Co I 6 Va Cav CSA
    Elizabeth A. 12 Oct 1845 - 4 Oct 1931

GRASTY, James D. 4 Mar 1850 - 11 July 1922

GRAY, Ella ... see THOMPSON

HARRIS, Charles M. 25 Feb 1847 - 19 Nov 1918 father, husb of Margaret Victoria
    Margaret Victoria 17 Dec 1845 - 29 Mar 1916 mother, wife of Charles M.

HUDGINS, George W. 4 Feb 1839 - 8 May 1923 father, husb of Susie M.
    Susie M. 29 June 1872 - 11 Nov 1949 mother wife of George W.

JACOBS, Ann   12 Oct 1840 - 2 Sept 1918   wife of James Fife Lumsden

LUMSDEN, Ann Jacobs ... see JACOBS
    Annie A. 1 Nov 1871 - 29 Sept 1933 wife of E. J. Lumsden
    E. J. 1862 - 9 Mar 1939 husb of 1] Sarah F. and 2] Annie A.
    Infants of E.J. and Sarah F.
    James Fife 17 Jan 1841 - 24 Sept 1945 husb of Ann Jacobs Lumsden
    Sarah F. 7 Feb 1868 - 31 May 1894 wife of E. J. Lumsden and mother of
        infants

POWELL, Lillie Olivia 18 July 1885 – 1 Sept 1885

QUISENBERRY, Benjamin 10 Mar 1824 – 25 Jan 1903 husb of Elizabeth
    Daniel   17 Aug 1838 –14 May 1921
    Elizabeth   10 May 1823 – 2 Feb 1903
    G. W. 14 Jan 1876 – 12 Oct 1897
    S. C. 28 Mar 1840 – 15 Oct 1909

REYNOLDS, Charles Alfred 4 Apr 1882 – 10 Aug 1911 son of G.W. and M.J. Reynolds
    Eliza 2 Nov 1847 – 15 Feb 1918
    Ella G. 6 May 1838 – 30 Dec 1898
    Estelle Irine 27 Oct 1872 – 22 May 1911 dau of G.W. and M.J. Reynolds, wife
        of H.E. Tinder
    George Washington 15 Aug 1839 – 11 Feb 1919 father
    Jenera b & d 1 June 1900
    Maretta J. 15 Dec 1851 – 27 Jan 1940 wife of George W., mother of Charles A.

SMITH, Annie Dewey 9 May 1898 – 3 Aug 1898
    Annie E. 18 Nov 1843 – 17 July 1932
    Francis M. no dates Taylor's Co Va L.A. CSA

THOMPSON, Ella Gray 26 Dec 1848 – 6 Sept 1936 wife of John G. Thompson
    John G. 29 Mar 1838 – 10 May 1913 CSA husb of Ella Gray

TINDER, Alice May 30 June 1849 – 22 May 1924 wife of Thomas T.
    Estelle Irine   ... see REYNOLDS
    Herbert E. 3 Jan 1857 – 13 Oct 1940 husb of 1] Mildred H. and 2] Estelle I.
    Mildred H. 14 Dec 1857 – 12 Aug 1888 wife of H.E. Tinder
    Thomas T. 15 Aug 1850 – 16 Feb 1935 spouse of Alice May

WEBB, Alice R. Canady   ... see CANADY
    John Arthur 3 May 1845 – 6 Mar 1913

WRIGHT, Benjamin 3 Aug 1837 – 7 Jan 1915 father, husb of Columbia Wright
    Columbia 10 Sept 1841 – 26 Sept 1887 mother, wife of Benjamin Wright
    Cordelia H. 1847 – 1922
    Susie 28 Feb 1861 – 16 June 1897 wife of A.W. Biscoe

BETHEL CHURCH CEMETERY

DIRECTIONS: Corner Route 650 and Route 669

Earliest birth date: 1868
Earliest death date: 1941
Total number of marked graves: 31
Apparent number of unmarked graves: 22

BLUE RUN CHURCH CEMETERY

DIRECTIONS: On Route 20 West at corner of Route 655

WEBB, Jane d. 25 Feb 1903 age 43 years, thrown by her horse and buried where
        she was killed. A large tomb, hand lettered cement slab.

CHESTNUT GROVE BAPTIST CHURCH CEMETERY

Directions: West on Route 33 for 0.2 miles beyond
Route 657. Church is on left.

Earliest birthdate: 1865
Earliest deathdate: 1955
Total number of marked graves: 11 plus others unmarked

EHEART PENTACOSTAL CHURCH CEMETERY

DIRECTIONS: Route 33 West to Eheart Corners (Route 644)
Then continue on Route 33 for 0.5 miles to
church and cemetery on left.

Earliest birthdate: 1887
Earliest deathdate: 1961
Total number of tombstones: 30

EMMANUEL EPISCOPAL CEMETERY OF RAPIDAN

DIRECTIONS: Cemetery is on Route 615/627 0.8 miles
inside Orange County from the Rapidan
River. It is also called the "Rapid Ann
Cemetery".

FITZHUGH, John Stuart 1834 – 1893
    Susan Pannill 1 Mar 1849 – 18 May 1913 mother

MOORE, Ella 15 Apr 1849 – 25 Feb 1897

PANNILL, Susan ... see FITZHUGH

PHILLIPS , Virginia H. 7 Feb 1836 – 10 May 1917 wife of Reuben Phillips

QUANN,Grace May 20 Jan 1898 – 29 July 1899 dau of J. H. and M. E. Quann

HOPEWELL BAPTIST CHURCH CEMETERY

DIRECTIONS: Route 20 West to Route 628 North for 2.7 miles
to church on left.

DAVIS, Helen McIntosh 1880 – 1900

McINTOSH, Cora 1856 – 29 Dec 1921 wife and mother
    Helen ... see DAVIS
    James 1850 – 1875

McINTOSH, William [Rev.] 17 Aug 1848 - 16 Feb 1942 Builder and Pastor of
            Hopewell Baptist Church for 35 years

WASHINGTON, Judy 2 Aug 1832 - 15 Mar 1904 wife of Chas. Washington

KNIGHTS CHAPEL CHURCH OF THE BRETHERN CEMETERY

DIRECTIONS: Route 33 West to Route 678 then South on Route
             777 to cemetery and church on left at county
             line. Cemetery is in Orange County and church
             appears to be in Albemarle County.

Earliest birthdate: 1860
Earliest deathdate: 1940
Total number of tombstones: 17 with at least 10 unmarked graves

MT CALVARY CHURCH CEMETERY

DIRECTIONS: Route 20 West to Route 600 South for 0.1 miles
             to church on left, cemetery on right.

Earliest birthdate: 1853
Earliest deathdate: 1943
Total number of tombstones: 66 plus many unmarked graves

MT HOLY CHURCH CEMETERY

DIRECTIONS: Route 522 North to Route 621 West for 0.1
             miles to church and cemetery at end of road.

Earliest birthdate: 1855
Earliest deathdate: 1910
Total number of tombstones: 37 plus some unmarked

MT HOREB UNITED METHODIST CHURCH CEMETERY

DIRECTIONS: From Orange Route 15 South to Route 639 East
             for 5.3 miles to church and cemetery on left.

BELL, James R. 20 Aug 1838 - 22 Sept 1912 husb of M. E. Bell
   M. E. 6 Jan 1839 - 15 July 1921 wife of James R. Bell

COLLINS, Lewis Richard 1848 - 1932

COOPER, Mary A. 1845 - 1936

GILLUM, Thos Mann 9 May 1823 - 18 Sept 1906 married 27 May 1856 celebrated
              Golden Wedding Anniversary 27 May 1906 [No wife
              given]

MATTHEWS, Martha 3 June 1845 - 20 Oct 1934 wife of William Matthews
     William 7 July 1835 - 15 Oct 1915 husb of Martha Matthews

MICHIE, Sarah T. 22 Nov 1823 - 8 June 1905

PAYNE, James M 17 Apr 1843 - 2 Aug 1914 beside Mary E.
     Mary Elizabeth 23 Feb 1847 - 12 Feb 1936 beside James M.

ROBERTSON, Ann Eliza 1848 - 1921 wife of Richard Robertson
     Richard 16 Nov 1848 - 4 Mar 1919 husb of Ann Eliza Robertson

MT LEBANON CHURCH CEMETERY

DIRECTIONS: Route 33 West to Route 644 South 1.8 miles
             to church and cemetery on right.

EDWARDS, Clementine Simpson 23 Aug 1850 - 6 Apr 1927 wife of Nathaniel J.
     Nathaniel J. 21 July 1854 - 5 Dec 1929 husb of Clementine S.

SIMPSON, Clementine ... see EDWARDS

Total number of tombstones: 19 plus 6 unmarked graves

MT OLIVE CHURCH CEMETERY

DIRECTIONS: Route 20 West to Route 624. South for 2.5 miles.

Earliest birthdate: 1854
Earliest deathdate: 1903
Total number of tombstones: 16 plus numerous unmarked graves

MT PISGAH CHURCH CEMETERY

DIRECTIONS: Route 20 West to Route 611 North to corner of
             Route 672.

CLAY, Henry 1840 - 1932

WRIGHT, James d. Mar 1923 age 80 years

Total number of tombstones: 62 plus 30 native stones, 60 destroyed under-
                 takers' markers and many unmarked graves

MT PLEASANT BAPTIST CHURCH CEMETERY

DIRECTIONS: On Route 629 2 miles West of Route 669

Earliest birthdate: 1855
Earliest deathdate: 1939
Total number of tombstones: 22 plus 8 unmarked graves

MT SINAI BAPTIST CHURCH CEMETERY

DIRECTIONS: On Route 20 near intersection of Route 624,
             Route 650, and Route 741

Earliest birthdate: 1870
Earliest deathdate: 1924
Total number of tombstones: 19

MT ZION BAPTIST CHURCH CEMETERY

DIRECTIONS: On Route 614 3.8 miles Northeast of Route 611

Earliest birthdate: 1891
Earliest deathdate: 1966
Total number of tombstones: 12

NEW HOPE BAPTIST CHURCH CEMETERY

DIRECTIONS: Route 20 West to Route 604 to Route 621. Near
             Gold Dale and 1.2 miles East of Mine Run.

ADAMS, Maggie ... see DULIN

CAMMACK, Flora May 1867 – 1891
     George W. 1 Nov 1836 – 17 Aug 1878 husb of Mary Jane Pidgeon
     Mary Jane Pidgeon ... see PIDGEON
     Nellie R. 4 Feb 1860 – 8 Oct 1895 wife of L. T. Lancaster

CHARLES, Hannah Pidgeon ... see PIDGEON

CHEWNING, A. H. 3 Sept 1833 – 23 Feb 1923 father, husb of Madora A.
     Madora A. 29 Aug 1853 – 13 July 1913 wife of A.H. Chewning

DAVIS, Charlotte S. 1864 – 1901
     Laura S. d. 27 Jan 1896

DAVIS, Lewis S. 1894 - 1896

DULIN, Amelia Roberta 13 Dec 1845 - 29 June 1921 wife of J.A. Dulin
    J. A. 29 Mar 1841 - 24 June 1908
    Maggie 20 Mar 1878 - 31 Dec 1892 wife of C.L. Adams

FAULCONER, Malinda 1829 - 1915 wife of Weedon Wiltshire

HERNDON, Amanda L. 15 Sept 1841 - 5 Oct 1923 wife of R.A.Herndon
    E. F. no dates Co F 1 Bn Va Res CSA
    Infant b & d 16 Mar 1892 child of Claude and Jessie Herndon
    Lucy Sleet 15 May 1845 - 26 Nov 1948
    Richard A. 10 Apr 1851 - 24 Sept 1926 husb of Amanda L.

JONES, Children of Mary Ann King and Churchill Jones
    Churchill 22 Jan 1820 - 24 Feb 1893 husb of Mary Ann King, Va Pvt Co B
                47 Reg Inf Arm CSA
    Mary Ann King 10 May 1830 - 20 Mar 1892 wife of Churchill

KING, Mary Ann ... see JONES

KNIGHTON, Anna K. d. 2 Feb 1926 age 79 yrs mother
    Estelle no dates beside John T.
    John T. 14 July 1849 - 23 Sept 1926 beside Estelle Va Cav CSA

LANCASTER, Adaline T. 19 June 1837 - 7 Jan 1912 wife of William
    Ella S. 27 Aug 1847 - 21 June 1926 mother, wife of Richard O.
    George E. 1848 - 1908
    Joseph M. 27 Apr 1845 - 18 Feb 1933
    Lucian T. 24 Dec 1868 - 13 Mar 1935
    Mary E. 16 July 1820 - 11 Dec 1892
    Nellie R. Cammack ... see CAMMACK
    Richard O. 19 Apr 1848 - 25 Mar 1940 father, husb of Ella S. Lancaster
    William T. d. 24 Sept 1930 husb of Adaline T.

MASON, Sallie E. 28 Dec 1876 - 6 Feb 1898 wife of Charles P. Webb
    William T. 28 May 1855 - 10 June 1900
    W. T. 28 May 1859 - 10 June 1900 [May be a second stone for WilliamT.]

OAKES, Thomas M. 1843 - 1931

PIDGEON, Hannah 14 Mar 1836 - 14 June 1908 wife of W. R. Charles
    Mary Jane 1832 - 1916 wife of George W. Cammack

SIMPSON, Eliza J. 2 Apr 1839 - 4 Mar 1910 beside Hugh M.
    Hugh M. no dates Co F 1 Va Res CSA beside Eliza J.

SLEET, Lucy ... see HERNDON

SUTHERLAND, Ada Z. d. 27 Aug 1913 2nd wife of Richard W. Sutherland
    Richard W. d. 7 June 1913 husb of 1] Virginia L and 2] Ada Z.
    Virginia L. d. 22 Aug 1892 wife of Richard W. Sutherland

SWIFT, Elizabeth J. 29 June 1834 - 22 Jan 1918

WEBB, Benjamin Rosser 29 Jan 1855 - 5 Feb 1906
    Betty M. 1847 - 1923
    Charles P. 8 Sept 1876 - 14 Jan 1937 husb of Sallie E.
    Sallie E. ... see MASON

WILTSHIRE, Asalea D. 27 Nov 1857 - 10 Jan 1891 wife of R. L. Wiltshire,
                    mother of Jessie O. and Grace E.
    Cassie J. 8 Aug 1900 - 31 Oct 1900
    Grace E. 16 Dec 1882 - 7 Mar 1896 dau of R.L. and A.D. Wiltshire

WILTSHIRE, Jessie O. 16 Jan 1889 - 26 July 1890 child of R.L. and A.D.
          Wiltshire
  Malinda Faulconer ... see FAULCONER
  Martha R. 27 Aug 1869 - 31 May 1960 wife of R.L. Wiltshire
  R. L. 5 Oct 1855 - 4 June 1937 husb of 1] Asalea D. and 2] Martha R.
  Silas P. 17 Sept 1897 - 21 Dec 1897

NORTH PAMUNKEY CHURCH CEMETERY

          DIRECTIONS: Route 669 to Route 629 West for 1 mile. Church
                       is on left.

BROCKMAN, Bettie T. 17 Apr 1837 - 25 June 1913 wife of Wm A. Brockman
                     "In memory of grandmother by W. A. and M. A. Brockman
  Edward T. 11 Feb 1858 - 17 Dec 1930 husband
  M. Alice Cooke d. 29 Apr 1928 age 74 years wife of Edward T.

BULLOCK, Annie D. 10 Nov 1834 - 22 Apr 1892

BURRUSS, Lancelot 2 Feb 1843 - 27 Aug 1916

CHESLEY, Mary Althea 5 Aug 1825 - 24 May 1904 Relict of William S. Chesley
                     mother
  Mary Somerville 1 May 1860 - 31 May 1935 wife of Walker John Decker

COLEMAN, Huldah Frazier 10 Oct 1851 - 10 Mar 1940 wife of Nicholas Penn
          Coleman
  John Chew no dates   Crenshaw's Btry Pegram's Lt Arty CSA
  L. L. no dates Ellett's Co Va Lt Atry CSA
  Nicholas Penn d. 16 May 18[7?]6 age 29 years only son of John P. Coleman

COOKE, M. Alice ... see BROCKMAN

DAVIS, P. B. 29 Aug 1841 - 10 Apr 1916

DECKER, Alexina Frazer 27 June 1844 - 13 June 1911 wife of Richard C.
  Apphia Ellen 8 May 1835 - 25 Mar 1910 wife of M.E. Decker
  M. E. 2 Feb 1834 - 13 Apr 1909 CSA husb of Apphia Ellen
  Mary Somerville Chesley ... see CHESLEY
  Richard C. 1 June 1843 - 26 Dec 1934
  Walker John 25 May 1841 - 2 Dec 1928

FRAZER, Alexina ... see DECKER
  David McCoy 17 July 1842 - 26 Mar 1926
  Don d. 24 Dec 1876 age 27 yrs only son Rev. Herndon Frazer
  Emily Irene 25 July 1848 - 8 Dec 1940 wife of David McCoy Frazer
  Herndon [Rev.] d. 10 July 1877 age 85 years father of Don Frazer, husb of
          Martha L. Frazer
  John 4 May 1837 - 6 Dec 1902 father
  Laura ... see MORTON
  Lucy ... see TERRILL
  Martha L. 24 June 1812 - 28 Nov 1888 wife of Rev. Herndon Frazer
  Susan Morton 30 May 1848 - 17 Feb 1926 wife of John
  William S. 13 Feb 1850 - 20 May 1911

FRAZIER, Huldah ... see COLEMAN

GOODWIN, Caroline D. 17 July 1830 - 8 Apr 1925
  John W. 27 Sept 1825 - 26 Feb 1886

JONES, H. Broaddus 19 Dec 1893 - 18 May 1898 son of H.P. and L.A. Jones

KENDALL, F. M. 18 June 1832 - 21 Nov 1909 husb of Isabelle
    Isabelle 27 Dec 1856 - 21 Nov 1916 wife of F. M. Kendall

McALISTER, Sarah E. 1 Jan 1853 - 29 Mar 1931 wife of W.B. McAlister
    W. B. 25 Dec 1848 - 29 Feb 1924 my husband

MORTON, George W. 12 Apr 1845 - 29 July 1918 husb of Laura F.
    Laura Frazer 1854 - 1884 wife of George W. Morton
    Susan ... see FRAZER
    Susie Laura 1878 - 1883 dau of George W. and Laura Frazer Morton

PINKARD, Mary Ann 12 Apr 1816 - 21 July 1914 age 98 years born in Culpeper
    County, Virginia

QUISENBERRY, Bettie E. 23 Aug 1831 - 15 Mar 1913

TERRILL, Lucy Frazer 26 Aug 1843 - 22 July 1932 wife of Oliver Towles Terrill
    Oliver Towles 15 June 1837 - 14 Sept 1932

VASS, William P. 22 Feb 1827 - 9 Jan 1899

WALKER, Adelia M. 27 Oct 1850 - 8 Dec 1931 sister

ORANGE GROVE CHURCH CEMETERY

DIRECTIONS: Route 522 South to Route 629 East to fork.
Continue on Route 629 to Route 653 for 1.5
miles to church on left just inside county
line.

Earliest birthdate: 1858
Earliest deathdate: 1926
Total number of tombstones: 36 plus 15 native stones and 10 unmarked graves

PALMYRA UNITED METHODIST CHURCH CEMETERY

DIRECTIONS: Route 522 North to Route 663 to church and
cemetery on left.

BRYANT, Anne d. 16 Sept 1910 age 57 wife of John Bryant
    John d. 26 July 1896 age 57 years husb of Anne

CONWAY, Fannie P. 1848 - 1924 same stone as John Eliason Conway
    George W. d. 23 Mar 1912 age 33 years son of P.S. and F.P. Conway
    John Eliason Killed in France 6 Oct 1918 same stone as Fannie P. Conway

ELIASON, Susan d. 16 Feb 1911 age 40 years wife of William E. Eliason
    William E. 11 Nov 1851 - 8 July 1893 age 41 years 7 months 27 days husb of
        Susan

FAULCONER, W. Taylor d. 28 Dec 1893 19 months son of Willard and Mamie
        Faulconer

HUME, John Randolph 26 April 1897 - 4 Nov 1899
    Lewis W. 15 Dec 1850 - 12 Apr 1927
    Martha B. 3 Nov 1858 - 3 Mar 1942 wife of Lewis W.

MARTIN, Alfred d. 8 Jan 1901 age 63 years
    Katie d. 18 Sept 1893 age 17 years
    Lucy A. d. 6 Aug 1911 age 74 years

PANNILL, Charlotte L. 1824 - 1899 beside George W.
    George W. 1847 - 1930 Co C 39 Va Cav CSA   beside Charlotte L.

WALLER, Luther B. 30 Sept 1835 - 10 July 1904 68 years 10 months 10 days

PILGRIM BAPTIST CHURCH CEMETERY

DIRECTIONS: From Wilderness Corner (Route 20 and Route 3)
             1.4 miles West on Route 3. Turn right for
             0.2 miles to cemetery on right behind church.

Earliest birthdate: 1863
Earliest deathdate: 1941
Total number of marked graves:14 plus numerous unmarked graves

RHOADSVILLE BAPTIST CHURCH CEMETERY

DIRECTIONS: Route 20 West to Route 741 West. Church is on
             left, has serpentine wall and is beautifully kept.

BEAZLEY, Sallie Morton d. 20 Oct 1924 age 101 years

BISCOE, Sallie ... see CHEWNING

BLEDSOE, William J. 1832 - 1920 CSA

BOND, Joseph W. 1835 - 1922 husb of Virginia Ann
    Virginia Ann 1830 - 1901 wife of Joseph W.

BRITTON, Virginia S. 2 Jan 1838 - 14 Apr 1924

BROWN, James F. d. 1892
    John W. 1847 - 1908

CAMMACK, Maria T. ... see DUVAL

CARPENTER, Anna E. 8 Mar 1840 - 22 Sept 1903 "Our Mother" wife of Horace T.
        Carpenter
    Horace T. 18 May 1843 - 7 Sept 1913 "Our Father" husb of Anna E.

CHEWNING, Sallie Biscoe 29 May 1846 - 22 Nov 1922 mother

CLARK, George A. 16 July 1840 – 3 July 1919
    J. J. 1810 – 1892   husb of Joy
    John William 9 Feb 1843 – 10 Oct 1928   husb of Susan M.
    Joy 1828 – 1900 wife of J.J. Clark
    Lucy d. 1898
    Susan M. 1848 – 1923 wife of John William
    William Thomas 17 Aug 1880 – 31 Mar 1892 son of J.W. and S.M. Clark

CLUFF, Edward 1828 – 1897 husb of Mary S.
    Mary S. 1830 – 1897 wife of Edward

COOPER, Margaret Jane 30 Apr 1842 – 3 Aug 1919 mother, wife of A.H. Cooper

CROMPTON, James no dates "In Memory of James Crompton, Confederate Soldier,
                   member of Jenkins Brigade of S.C."

DUVAL, Maria Theodora Cammack 10 June 1814 – 2 Jan 1900 wife of Robert Alex-
              ander Duval

FAULCONER, James William 1847 – 1924 father beside Lillie E. R.
    Lillie E. Reynolds 1856 – 1933 mother beside James W.

GOOCH, Minnie A. 21 Feb 1848 – 9 Dec 1904 wife of William E. Gooch
    William E. 19 Oct 1851 – 21 Oct 1922 husb of Minnie A. Gooch

HATCH, Eugene B. 27 June 1870 – 20 Mar 1900
    Mary L. 18 Mar 1838 – 24 Jan 1890 wife of Thomas J. Hatch
    Thomas J. 18 June 1836 – 25 Sept 1917 CSA husb of Mary L.
    Willie H. d. 3 May 1880   age 19 years son of T. J. and M. L. Hatch

HERNDON, John B. 11 Oct 1845 – 28 Feb 1912 CSA husb of Sarah E.
    Sarah E. 15 Aug 1842 – 29 Nov 1900 married 21 Dec 1865 to John B. Herndon

JAMES, J.W. 1822 – 1892 father, CSA husb of Lucy S.
    Lucy S. Keith 1841 – 1924 mother, wife of J.W.

JEFFRIES, Mary M. 17 Nov 1847 – 17 Aug 1920

KEELING, Ella ... see TINDER

KEITH, Lucy S. ... see JAMES

KNIGHTON, Grace Irene 24 Aug 1898 – 17 Dec 1900
    Mabel 11 Aug 1883 – 22 Nov 1895
    Roderick H. 31 July 1848 – 29 Oct 1901

LEE, William Harvey 6 Oct 1813 – 3 Jan 1901

MANN, Annie Cleveland 16 Sept 1884 – 22 Nov 1886 same stone with Estelle Jamie
                           Mann
    Estelle Jamie 14 July 1881 – 22 Nov 1886 same stone as Annie Cleveland Mann
    Jas J. 9 June 1850 – 28 Jan 1917 between Sara J. and Mabel E.
    Mabel E. 14 Sept 1851 – 20 Feb 1944 beside Jas J.
    Sara J. 28 Oct 18[9?] – 3 Dec 1897 beside Jas J.

McCORD, Cornelia 1850 – 1928 mother, wife of Daniel G. McCord
    Daniel G. 1854 – 1909 father, husb of Cornelia
    Samuel A. 1845 – 1925
    Susie 1875 – 1876

MORTON, Sallie ... see BEAZLEY

REYNOLDS, Lillie ,,, see FAULCONER

ROW, James W. 19 Jan 1840 – 19 Oct 1901 beside Jane B.
    Jane B. d. 11 July 1923 mother, beside James W.

SANDERS, Mollie E. 5 Nov 1862 – 24 Mar 1920 wife of W.P.Sanders
    William Preston 26 Sept 1846 – 20 Feb 1921

SIZER, J. M. [Rev.] 1848 – 1922 husb of Nellie V.
    Nellie V. 1850 – 1934 wife of Rev. J.M. Sizer

SOMERVILLE, John H. 22 Oct 1823 – 28 Apr 1881
    Sarah Elizabeth 13 Jan 1833 – 20 Feb 1918

THAYER, Angeline K. 20 Sept 1847 – 10 Aug 1934 wife of John S. Thayer
    John S. 21 Oct 1845 – 30 Nov 1920

TINDER, Ella Keeling 9 July 1853 – 25 Mar 1897 beside John S.
    Ella Keeling 1896 – 1898
    John Spencer 30 Nov 1848 – 8 Dec 1926 beside Ella K.

TRUMBO, L. C. 11 Dec 1833 – 7 June 1919

TUCKER, John W. 4 Aug 1850 – 2 Oct 1926   beside Mollie H.
    Mollie H. 31 Dec 1862 – 5 Nov 1925 beside John W.

WATKINS, Mary E. 13 June 1819 – 4 Oct 1903

WAUGH, Ellen C. 16 Aug 1839 – 16 Oct 1916 "Our Mother" wife of Robert Goree
    Waugh
    Goree 19 May 1789 – 20 Feb 1872 "Our Grandfather"
    Robert Goree 12 Oct 1828 – 17 July 1906 "Our Father" husb of Ellen C.
    Pvt Va Lt Art CSA

ST THOMAS CHURCH CEMETERY OF ORANGE

> DIRECTIONS: Route 20 bypass to Orange. Cemetery is at
> back of church and consists of two crypts and
> a row of eleven headstones against the wall.
> This location for the headstones is to prevent
> vandalism.

BOULWARE, Mary 11 Nov 1835 – 29 Nov 1837
    Mary T. 11 Feb 1809 – 22 Apr 1859
    Thomas 6 Dec 1833 – 21 Nov 1837

DAVIS, John A.G. 23 Aug 1858 – 8 Jan 1862 only son of Rev. G. T. and Mrs.
    A. M. Davis

GULLEN, Louis W. 26 July 18 [5?] 9 – 20 Apr 1860 son of George and M.S. Gullen
    M. S. 27 Mar 1810 – 10 Mar 1860

HACKNEY, Richard d. 1837 age 28 years

HANSBOROUGH, Alexander Hamilton 1807 – 1846

LIPSCOMB, Robert 13 June 1800 – 22 July 1842 [crypt]

RANDOLPH Roberta M 25 Dec 1837 – 19 Sept 1863 dau of Charles and Mary Randolph
    of Faquier County, Virginia

WILLIAMSON, Joseph A. d. 14 Aug 1853 age 48

WILSON, Robert d. 13 Mar 1839 in 80th year of his age "Sacred to the Memory of
Robert Wilson, a native of Renfrewshire, Scotland,
but for the last fifty years a resident of Orange County,
Virginia, by whose inhabitants he was highly respected
and beloved. He died March 13, 1839 in the 80th year
of his age." [crypt]

WOLFLEY, John 10 Sept 1819 – 1 Aug 1837
Richard H. 16 Oct 1817 – 11 July 1840

SALEM UNITED METHODIST CHURCH CEMETERY

DIRECTIONS: Route 20 West near Route 621

FOULKS, Harry P. 1878 – 1879 son of W.H. and L.P. Foulks
Lavina P. 9 Mar 1858 – 5 May 1949 mother of Harry P., wife of Wm H. Foulks
William H. 22 Dec 1850 – 28 Mar 1900 father of Harry P., husb of Lavina P.

HATCH, _____ 11 Mar 1806 – 17 Dec 18__
Henry 6 Oct 1805 – 29 Dec _____

HERNDON, William A. 27 July 1899 – 11 Aug 1899

HICKS, William B. 2 Jan 1804 – 12 July 1894

JOHNSON, John W. 17 Dec 1844 – 12 Feb 1918 CSA beside Louise K.
Louise K. 24 June 1842 – 2 Sept 1887 beside John W.

KUBE, Catherine E. 17 May 1836 – 7 Apr 1923 wife of Archilles Rhoades
John B. d. 22 Apr 1937 Pvt Va Inf CSA

RHOADES, Archilles 6 July 1835 – 17 May 1905 husb of Catherine E.K.
Catherine E. Kube ... see KUBE
Nancy 8 Jan 1801 – 17 Apr 1899

SEELY, J. 1848 – 1921 beside S.C.H.Seely
S.C.H. 1854 – 1932 beside J. Seely

WEBB, Martha J. 14 Dec 1841 – 2 Apr 1922

SHADY GROVE BAPTIST CHURCH CEMETERY

[FOR FORMER MINISTERS OF CHURCH]

DIRECTIONS: Route 612 West to Route 677. This cemetery
is just behind the church and consists of a
cinder block fenced area without a gate. All
tombstones appear below.

BURRUSS, J.H. [Rev.] 10 Sept 1850 – 3 May 1923 "Dowby SDL Union"

DAVIS, Edith Elizabeth d. 14 July 195_ age 65 years wife of Rev. G.L.Davis
G.L. [Rev.] 4 Jan 1886 – 14 June 1947 Pastor for 32 years, husb of Edith E.

JOHNSON, Philip   1834 - 23 January 1927

PRESSLEY, J.H. [Rev.] 26 Sept 1858 - 27 Apr 1914 Missionary to Africa 1883
                      Member and ex-pastor Shady Grove Baptist Church

SHADY GROVE BAPTIST CHURCH CEMETERY

DIRECTIONS: Corner Route 612 and Route 677. Note: 48
              graves are in a line near edge of cemetery
              toward woods. Many of these look new, but
              bear older dates, as if the cemetery had
              been moved recently. Also they are buried
              in chronological order with the earliest
              death date nearest the road. Families are
              not buried together in this part of cemetery.

RICHARDSON, Mary L. 1849 - 29 October 1959 age "112"

_____, Lou W.   ___Ju_____ -   age 104 years stone very weathered

Total number of marked graves: 92, unmarked 37, few marked by native
                    stones.

UNION GROVE CHRISTIAN CHURCH CEMETERY

DIRECTIONS: Route 33 West to Route 644 North for short
              distance to church and cemetery on left.

BIRCKHEAD, Annie V. 16 Feb 1877 - 23 May 1962 wife of Thomas E.
          Thomas E. 27 Feb 1872 - 5 July 1949
          Virginia L. 29 Sept 1897 - 7 July 1899 dau of T. E. and A.V. Birckhead

Earliest birthdate: 1856
Total number of tombstones: 58

UNIONVILLE CHRISTIAN CHURCH CEMETERY

DIRECTIONS: From intersection of Route 522 and Route 20
              take Route 671 to church on left. Walled
              cemetery is behind church.

BASTRESS, Cora M. 1868 - 1892

BICKLEY, Tomasia Myrtle ... see PERRY

BOSTON, Sophia S. ... see PERRY

BOSTON, Sophia Thomas 11 Sept 1880 - 27 Feb 1892

BROCKMAN, Nannie ... see HARRELL

CAMPBELL, Mary P. 1890 - 1892

CLARK, Guy 1898 1 day old

GOULDMAN, Virginia 9 Jan 1836 - 10 Feb 1910 wife of J.R. Gouldman

HARRELL, Nannie Brockman 1 May 1847 - 28 Mar 1931 wife of Theodore Leith
                           Harrell
         Theodore Leith no dates husb of Nannie B., Co H 6th Va Cav CSA

HOPKINS, Harriet 1841 - 30 Oct 1919 mother, wife of Zebulon
         Jane J. 6 Nov 1850 - 21 Feb 1936 wife of Marshall Hopkins
         Marshall no dates husb of Jane J., 28th Va Inf
         Zebulon no dates husb of Harriet Co I 6th Va Cav CSA

HUGHES, Mary E. 10 June 1847 - 14 Jan 1918

LEE, Edward d. Sept 1889
     Susan 1820 - 1894

LUCK, Ella S. 17 Nov 1857 - 17 Sept 1954 beside Wm A. Luck
      William A. 1 Feb 1834 - 26 Sept 1886 beside Ella S. Luck

MARTIN, Edmonia 1878 - 1891
        Elizabeth P. 1841 - 1907
        Emma J. Waugh 10 Nov 1854 - 22 Dec 1942 mother, wife of W. J. Martin
        Henry K. 27 Jan 1852 - 7 Oct 1928 husb of Lissie May
        Hollis R. 30 June 1876 - 7 Nov 1899 son of W.J. and Emma Martin
        Josephine C. 1883 - 1885
        Lewis A. 6 Feb 1850 - 7 Jan 1934
        Lissie May 13 Oct 1856 - 2 June 1898 wife of H.K. Martin
        Oliva C. 1886 - 1887
        W. J. 29 Oct 1849 - 21 Jan 1923 husb of Emma J.
        Warren D. 1896 - 1898
        William Elmore 1892 - 1892
        William H. 1818 - 1892

McCord, Jacob S. 3 Sept 1847 - 20 Aug 1923

PERRY, Elijah Richard 19 May 1840 - 29 Mar 1929 Evangelist Minister, husb of
                       Sophia S. B., son of George L. and Mary [Polly]
                       Brown Perry. Married 2] Tomasia M. Bickley
       Sophia Boston 23 Oct 1845 - 7 Nov 1888 1st wife of Elijah R. Perry, dau of
                       John P. and Jane Frances Waugh Boston
       Tomasia Myrtle Bickley 1858 - 1948 2nd wife of Elijah R. Perry

STRONG, Rebecca A. 1844 - 1916 wife beside Robert C.
        Robert C. 1837 - 1907 beside Rebecca

SWAIN, John Henry 7 Sept 1835 - 24 Oct 1911 Co K Regmt Va Inf CSA, husb of
                   Mollie W.
       Mollie W. 1840 - 1915 wife of John H.

TALLEY, Malinda B. 1 Oct 1838 - 2 Oct 1908

THOMAS, Sophia ... see BOSTON

WAUGH, Emma Jane ... see MARTIN

WILLOUGHBY, Arrabella Ann 16 May 1848 - 10 Oct 1914 wife of Thomas S.

WILLOUGHBY, Thomas S. 12 Nov 1840 – 17 Apr 1892 husb of Arrabella A.
Willoughby

WADDELL PRESBYTERIAN CHURCH CEMETERY

DIRECTIONS: On Route 615/627 0.2 miles East of the Rapidan
River crossing

ALEXANDER, Mildred Morton 12 Mar 1877 – 21 May 1890 dau of James P. and
Annie A. Alexander

ARMENTROUT, Amanda M. 21 Oct 1833 – 4 June 1909 wife of B.F. Armentrout
B. F. 23 May 1833 – 13 Dec 1919 son of David Armentrout

BLEDSOE, Rachel ... see McCLARY

BROWNING, Phillip Jones 17 May 1870 – 25 Apr 1953 husband
Sallie Busby 10 Nov 1880 – 22 Apr 1963 wife of Phillip Jones Browning, dau
of Alice Lucas and William Thomas Busby

BUSBY, Alice Lucas 9 Dwv 1856 – 9 Mar 1925 mother, wife of Wm Thomas Busby,
[inscription on back of Phillip J. and Sally B. Brown-
ing stone]
Sallie ... see BROWNING
William Thomas 15 Sept 1850 – 1 July 1882 father, husb of Alice L. [inscrip-
tion on back of Phillip J. and Sally B. Browning stone]

CARTER, Thomas B. 1 Apr 1859 – 26 May 1875 son of Robert M. and E. M. Carter
born in Nomony, Mississippi died Mount Sharon, Virginia

FERGUSON, Marjory B. 28 Jan 1845 – 15 Apr 1926 born in Bunfermline, Scotland

GREENE, John Peyton 22 May 1869 – 28 Apr 1874 son of John L. and M. Genevieve Greene

GRIMES, Genevieve Peyton 18 Mar 1842 – 11 Feb 1928 wife of J. Lee Grimes
J. Lee d. 12 Jan 1879 age 34 years 6 months 2 days husb of Genevieve P.

HAMILTON, Jeanie ... see SOMERVILLE

HENDERSON [large monument no headstones or markers]

HOLLADAY, Elizabeth Minor 1 Dec 1891 – 21 Dec 1894 dau of Lewis Littlepage and
Mary Love Minor Holladay
Fannie 11 Feb 1876 – 16 May 1901 wife of Henry Thompson Holladay
Frances Porter 5 Aug 1836 – 22 Jan 1917 wife of W.T. Holladay
Henry Thompson 16 Aug 1828 – 22 Feb 1910 husb of Fannie
James Porter 26 Mar 1867 – 6 Sept 1892
Julia Minor 12 Feb 1866 – 26 Mar 1871 dau of Henry T. and Fannie W.
Lewis Littlepage 1 July 1863 – 6 June 1925 husband
Mary Isabelle 26 Aug 1841 – 5 Mar 1927 wife of Waller Lewis Holladay
Mary Love Minor 15 Mar 1864 – 15 Nov 1945 wife of Lewis Littlepage Holladay
Waller Lewis 22 Mar 1830 – 19 Apr 1906

JENKINS, Edwin Wyatt 4 Apr 1852 – 26 June 1896

JONES, Ann Barbara d. 15 Jan 1877 age 60 yrs dau of Laney and Martha Jones

JURGESEN, Holger W.   6 Mar 1881 – 13 Nov 1898

LEWIS, Huldah ... see PEYTON

LUCAS, Alice ... see BUSBY

LUCKETT, Lucie P. ... see THORNTON
    Thornton 21 Apr 1876 – 10 May 1876 inf son of L.T. and L.J. Luckett

McCLARY, Charles L.   9 Dec 1840 – 13 July 1929
    Charles L. 14 Mar 1874 – 10 Feb 1900 brother
    James Garland 25 Feb 1844 – 27 Aug 1924 husb of Rachel
    Lucy V. 10 Apr 1842 – 28 Sept 1885 mother, wife of Charles L. McClary
    Musa Dora 26 Jan 1874 – 4 July 1891 dau of J. G. and Rachel McClary
    Rachel Bledsoe 14 Apr 1841 – 10 Nov 1926 wife of James Garland McClary,
        mother of Musa Dora

MINOR, John no dates Surgn Va Regt CSA
    John Bailey d. 21 Sept 1892
    Mary Love ... see HOLLADAY

PEYTON, Alice H. d. 12 June 1955 wife of John W. Peyton
    Genevieve ... see GRIMES
    George O. no dates Co A 13 Va Inf CSA husb of Huldah L.
    Huldah Lewis 12 Apr 1837 – 4 Aug 1904 wife of George O.
    John W. 5 Apr 1834 – 23 Apr 1914 husb of Alice H.
    Sarah Martha d. 7 Jan 1892 72 years, wife of John S. Peyton
    Willa Anna 11 Feb 1813 – 22 Mar 1891 wife of William S. Peyton
    William S. 4 Dec 1816 – 30 Jan 1899 husb of Willa Anna
    Willie Lewis 2 Nov 1872 – 17 Sept 1887 son of G. O. and Huldah Lewis Peyton

PORTER, Frances ... see HOLLADAY

SOMERVILLE, Jeanie Hamilton 15 May 1862 – 29 Jan 1917 wife of Samuel Wilson
        Somerville
    Mary Hamilton 30 June 1898 – 5 Jan 1899 dau of S.W. and J.H. Somerville
    Samuel Wilson 20 Aug 1859 – 9 Dec 1934 husb of Jeanie Hamilton

STEWART, Catherine 1846 – 1936
    William d. 7 Dec 1884 age 46 years

SYME, Robina ... see TAYLOR

TALIAFERRO, Wm R. no dates Co A 3 Va Inf CSA

TALLEY, Fannie A. 15 Dec 1834 – 29 Mar 1909

TAYLOR, Robina Syme no dates wife of William G. Taylor of Bunfermline,
        Scotland
    William G. no dates of Bunfermline, Scotland

THOMPSON, Martha Helen d. 26 April 1877 age 79 years

THORNTON, James 22 May 1841 – 14 June 1895 husb of Lucie P. Luckett

VAN LEAR, Permealia M. d. 10 Sept 1884 70 years 4 months 7 days wife of
        Robert Van Lear

WRIGHT, Frederick G. d. 12 Feb 1876 age 41 son of David Wright M.D. of
        County Wicklow, Ireland where he died of fever

WILDERNESS CHAPEL CEMETERY

DIRECTIONS: Route 20 West less than 0.1 miles to Route 701
on left. Sharp turn to gate of cemetery on
right. Chapel foundation and entryway still
visible, but remainder of chapel collapsed
a few years back.

ADAMS, Charles W. 1870 - 1888 same stone as Samuel F., Virginia C., and
Sallie B.
Sallie B. 1879 - 1920 see note above
Samuel F. 1848 - 1918 see note above
Virginia C. 1846 - 1899 see note above

DEMPSEY, Albert Sidney 9 May 1887 - 11 May 1889 fenced
Archie A. 21 Sept 1893 - 14 June 1894 in fenced plot
Arthur S. 3 Jan 1890 - 28 Mar 1891 in fenced plot
David 30 Sept 1850 - 22 July 1920 in fenced plot
Nancy E. d. 13 Mar 1902 in her 85th year mother, in fenced plot

JAMES, Ann ... see JOHNSON

JENNINGS, Robert A. 12 Apr 1848 - 22 May 1912 beside Willie J.
Willie J. 1855 - 1937 beside Robert A.

JOHNSON, Ann James d. 3 Feb 1901 83 years "She always made home happy"

KUPER, C.H. [Dr.] 30 May 1850 - 27 June 1907 beside Mary Ella
Charles L. 29 Sept 1887 - 29 Sept 1895
Mary Ella 1855 - 1934 mother, beside Dr. C. H. Kuper
T. Hunter 27 Oct 1889 - 7 Aug 1897
Vergie H. 21 Dec 1880 - 26 Aug 1937 wife of Wm C.
Wm C. 29 Mar 1875 - 10 Apr 1935 husb of Vergie H.

LACY, William Jones 4 Aug 1853 - 6 Jan 1884 born at Ellwood, died at Woodville

WRIGHT, Lizzie E. 7 May 1822 - 23 Sept 1899

ZION BAPTIST CHURCH CEMETERY

DIRECTIONS: Route 15 South to Route 639 East for 0.3 miles
to cemetery at Madison Run. Below are listed
all stones found at this church.

FITZGERALD, Effie D. 1903 - 1918

HICKS, Lucy M. 25 Apr 1851 - 4 May 1912 wife of Peter Wesley Hicks
Peter Wesley 16 May 1843 - 23 May 1908 husb of Lucy M. Hicks

RINER, Edgar M. 19 May 1871 - 12 June 1905 "Woodman of the World"

SCOTT, Huldah Jane 15 Nov 1846 - 21 Jan 1927 wife of Johnson Daniel Scott

SCOTT, Johnson Daniel 12 Apr 1851 – 15 Oct 1907 husb of Huldah Jane Scott

ZOAR BAPTIST CHURCH CEMETERY

DIRECTIONS: Route 20 West to Route 611 North for 2.6 miles
to church and cemetery on left.

ALMOND, Esther 10 Mar 1909 – 11 Mar 1909 also on family marker with Rena,
        Thomas J., Lucy, and Thomas Walter
    Lucy J. 25 Dec 1849 – 5 Apr 1931 see note above
    Rena 20 Oct 1880 – 4 July 1888   see note above
    Thomas J. 26 Mar 1842 – 5 Dec 1909 CSA also see note above
    Thomas Walter 18 Jan 1904 – 10 Jan 1906 see note above

BARTLEY, Nathan T. 2nd Lt Co C 7th Va Inf CSA, husb of Sarah E. no dates
    Sarah E. 3 June 1840 – 28 Sept 1904 wife of Nathan T.

CANADAY, Lulu V. 15 Dec 1879 – 16 Aug 1885 dau of A.A. and V.H. Canaday

HURLOCK, Jacob H. sr 18 Nov 1850 – 30 Aug 1914 husb of Laura M.
    Laura M. 29 Nov 1857 – 25 Feb 1947 wife of Jacob H. sr

JOHNSON, Bettie P. 1845 – 1925 beside J.M.
    Eva 1882 – 1895
    Irving 1875 – 1897
    J. Madison 1841 – 1927
    Rufus 19 June 1894 – 22 Nov 1895

MORRIS, Addie E. 9 Dec 1861 – 27 Dec 1938 mother, beside John L.
    James Harrison 1849 – 1935
    John L. 18 May 1848 – 9 Jan 1934 father, beside Addie E.

PAYNE, Charles 8 July 1832 – 1 Sept 1899 husb of Eliza J.T.
    Elizabeth C. 7 Nov 1831 – 5 Apr 1928 wife of Wm H.
    Eliza J. T. 22 Jan 1847 – 11 Sept 1891 wife of Charles
    James T. 27 Jan 1850 – 22 June 1851
    Mary Shadrach 24 Feb 1825 – 24 May 1854
    William H. 18 Jan 1819 – 28 Sept 1882 husb of Elizabeth C.

RHOADES, R. Wayne 29 Oct 1895 – 4 Dec 1895

SANDERS, John R. 3 May 1835 – 29 Aug 1923 father, husb of Mary A.
    Mary A. 16 Apr 1830 – 19 Apr 1901 mother, wife of John R.

SHADRACH, Mary ... see PAYNE

SMITH, William B. no dates Co C 7th Inf Va CSA

FAMILY CEMETERIES

* * *

ADAMS - ROWE FAMILY CEMETERY

DIRECTIONS: Route 20 West to last farm road on right before
              crossing Mine Run. This is the Robert Rhoades
              farm. Mrs. Rhoades, informant. There are no
              stones except for natural rocks. It is an old
              cemetery and belonged to the Adams - Rowe fam-
              ilies. Mrs Maude Welcher, postmistress at
              Mine Run might have information.

APPERSON FAMILY CEMETERY

DIRECTIONS: Route 20 West to Route 623 1.0 miles to end of
              road, turn left down overgrown farm road to
              small house on left. Mr Woodrow Apperson
              [b. 1917] will lead you to two cemeteries.
              The second one is the Herndon Family Cemetery.
              Both are through dense underbrush within 0.3
              miles of the house.

APPERSON, Joseph no dates, father of Lucy Apperson Herndon , great-grand-
                  father of informant
_____Tinder   wife of Joseph, mother of Lucy Apperson Herndon, great-grand-
                  mother of informant

AUMACK FAMILY CEMETERY

DIRECTIONS: Route 33 West to Route 658 South 1.5 miles to
              cemetery on right. POSTED! Go to house at end
              of road, approximately another 0.5 miles. Cemetery
              is fenced and overgrown.

AUMACK, John 1 April 1851 - 19 July 1933 husb of Sallie E.
    Katie Mozella 22 Oct 1877 - 24 Dec 1918 dau of John and Sallie Aumack
    Sallie E. 30 Sept 1852 - 26 Nov 1935 wife of John, mother of Katie M.

CLARKE, Garland J. 1856 - 1904

BAILEY - BATTAILLE FAMILY CEMETERY

DIRECTIONS: From Orange Route 615 North to Route 627 East to
Route 636 North for 3.7 miles. Right at second
drive beyond the paved portion of the road. Ask
permission at house. Cemetery is nicely kept with
a white board fence and is 0.1 miles up hill in
pasture.

BAILEY, John S. 7 Oct 1861 - 6 Dec 1912
Mary B. 10 May 1866 - 10 Mar 1936
Norris S. 14 Sept 1893 - 22 Mar 1923

BATTAILLE, Daughter 10 Oct 1891 - 10 July 1892
James 6 Feb 1872 - 1 Dec 1893 son of J.R. and B.
Jane I. 13 Apr 1844 - 13 Mar 1912 wife of J.R.
J.R. 8 Nov 1835 - 16 Feb 1923 CSA plaque husb of Jane I. and of B.
Leo Yates 7 Feb 1889 - 9 Oct 1958
M.W. 16 Oct 1870 - 8 June 1892 dau of J.R. and B.
Walter Raymond 17 Mar 1884 - 25 Aug 1945

YATES, Leo ... see BATTAILLE

BARBOURSVILLE FAMILY CEMETERY

DIRECTIONS: Route 33 West from Gordonsville to Route 678 West.
South on Route 777 for 0.4 miles to brick house
on right. Ask permission and directions to cemetery

BARBOUR, Anne W. 10 Nov 1817 - 25 Feb 1851 child of B.J. and C.H. Barbour
On obelisk with James. Front of marker: "Lovely and
pleasant in their lives and in their death they were not
divided" Footstone "AWB"
B. Johnson 14 June 1821 - 2 Dec 1894 husb of Caroline H.
Benjamin Johnson 10 Oct 1802 - 4 July 1820 second son of James and Lucy
Caroline H. 3 Feb 1825 - 21 July 1904 wife of B. Johnson Barbour
Caroline Homassel ... see ELLIS
Frances Cornelia d. 23 Aug 1802 age 14 mo 4 ds dau of James and Lucy
George Watson of "Hampstead" 8 Apr 1859 - 31 Jan 1937
James d. 7 July 1842 Pvt 39 Va Mil War of 1812 [Plaque placed by his
descendents to the sixth generation in 1930: "To the
Glory of God and in Loving Memory of James Barbour
1775 - 1842, Governor of Virginia 1812 - 1814, U.S.
Senator, Secretary of War, Minister to Great Britian,
Founder of the Literary Fund of Virginia, and in loving
memory of his wife, Lucy Maria Johnson 1775 - 1860."
James 5 Feb 1816 - 5 Jan 1851 son of B.J. and C.H. Barbour. See Anne W.
for inscription.
Lucy Maria Johnson 1775 - 1860 wife of James, Governor of Virginia
Nanny [see Anne W., thought to be a "pet" name for Anne]
Thomas 1854 - 1938

ELLIS, Caroline Homassel Barbour 8 Dec 1861 - 30 May 1943

JOHNSON, Lucy Maria ... see BARBOUR

TALIAFERRO, James Barbour 4 Feb 1826 - 31 Mar 1844 "To our Brother, son of
John Seymour Taliaferro and Lucy Maria Barbour, his
wife." [see p 62 TOMBSTONE INSCRIPTIONS OF
KING GEORGE COUNTY, VIRGINIA]
Lucy Maria 21 May 1823 - 29 Mar 1844 "To our Sister, oldest child of John
Seymour Taliaferro and his wife Lucy Maria Barbour."

"John T.Y." no information ?child?

BEALE CEMETERY

DIRECTIONS: Route 3 West to Flat Run. Cemetery is nearly
across from Flat Run General Store and West of
Lake-of-the-Woods. Inquire at store. Informants:
Mrs Day and Mr Jack J. Duval   There were only
natural stones. It is considered a "slave"
cemetery and consisted of approximately three
acres.   No burials since the Civil War according
to the informants.

BEALE'S LOT

DIRECTIONS: Route 20 West to Route 611 South to Route 604 South
to Route 608 South. Cemetery is across from
Sullivan's Store in deep woods. Can only be reached
on foot. Informant Keith Walters. No stones, but
evidence of many sunken unmarked graves.

BEGORRAH SLAVE CEMETERY

DIRECTIONS: Route 522 South to Route 629 East to Route 651 for
0.2 miles to farm on right. No stones. This was
the old "Emma Thompson Farm" and information may
be available from Mrs. Evelyn Barnes (Mrs. Clarence
Eugene). Informant: Magdalene B. Murphy, owner.

BISCOE FAMILY CEMETERY

DIRECTIONS: Route 20 West to Route 692 South to Route 651
where a jog to the left is an overgrown right
of way. Follow the old road for 0.8 miles to
fenced cemetery on right at end of road. Note:
There were 3 native stones and one unreadable
marker.

BISCOE, Thomas Lawson 6 Nov 1850 – 21 June 1940
    V.A. [Mrs.] 3 Sept 1854 – 2 Jan 1933

EDENTON, Edward Ellis 27 Sept 1910 – 3 July 1911

BLAKEY FAMILY CEMETERY

DIRECTIONS: Route 20 North from Barboursville to Route 665
West for 0.1 miles to cemetery at curve of road
on right.

BLAKEY, Arthur G. [M.D.] 8 Mar 1888 – 24 Apr 1963
    Charles W. 1890 – 1944
    Eleanor M. 25 Sept 1886 – 23 Mar 1908
    Ella J. 1861 – 1938 mother, wife of James W.
    George W. 9 Oct 1891 – 14 Aug 1941
    James H. 12 Apr 1883 – 21 Nov 1901
    James W. 6 June 1854 – 19 Mar 1941 father, husb of Ella J.
    Jessica C. 25 Aug 1893 – 11 Mar 1969
    Katus R. [Dr.] 10 Nov 1924 – 20 Aug 1975
    Louis P. 1893 – 1960
    Sarah Ann 17 Feb 1880 – 30 Mar 1912

CANIDAY, Mary 1828 – 1904

DUDLEY, Rosa B. 1878 – 1940 mother, beside Nellie D. Thomas

HARTZOG, Louise E. 5 Mar 1921 – 17 Aug 1950

HILL, George W. 13 Jan 1896 – 18 July 1941
    Mary A. 25 Sept 1881 – 15 Jan 1959

HINTON, Susie E. 1927 – 1955

ROBINSON, Louis W. jr 17 Mar 1945 – 23 Mar 1945

THOMAS, Nellie D. 1907 – 1941 beside Rosa B. Dudley

BLEDSOE FAMILY CEMETERY

DIRECTIONS: Route 20 West to Route 611 North, take first
road on left to SPRINGFIELD FARM owned by
H.C. Bledsoe. Note: There is also a slave
cemetery on this property, but it is without
markers. Informant:Clyde Johnson.

BLEDSOE, Lillian Sanders 22 June 1860 - 23 May 1920
   Mary 16 Oct 1872 - 5 Feb 1915
   Mary Cattlett Sanders 1833 [?] - 9 Apr 1895
   Moses Garnett 26 Mar 1834 - 20 Mar 1915 CSA
   Thomas Hansford 1866 [?] - 1898

HANSON, Rebecca ... see SANDERS

SANDERS, Lillian ... see BLEDSOE
   Mary Cattlett ... see BLEDSOE
   Rebecca Hanson 28 Sept 1828 - 22 Feb 1907

BLEDSOE'S CORNERS CEMETERIES

DIRECTIONS: Route 20 West to Route 522 North to Route 663
North to Route 622 at Palmyra Church East for
1.8 miles to first site then to corners to
site of second cemetery. Mrs. Harris who
lives across from second cemetery says both
were moved in 1973. She did not know where
they are presently located, nor the names.

SLAVE CEMETERY ON THE BLEDSOE FARM

DIRECTIONS: See Bledsoe Family Cemetery above for directions
and a note about this cemetery. Informant:
Clyde Johnson

BREEDEN FAMILY CEMETERY

DIRECTIONS: Route 20 West from Orange to Route 616 North to
Oak Chapel. Park. Permission from house on
corner before chapel. Cemetery is in field
across from chapel. It is fenced and well cared
for.

BREEDEN, Ada D. 25 Dec 1905 - 12 Dec 1958
Ada Kay 9 Nov 1969 - 6 Dec 1971 picture
Elizabeth d. 11 Jan 1947 18 years
Gilbert d. Feb 1948 age 13 yrs 29 das
Marie d. 30 Dec 1940
Paul Roosevelt d. 2 Apr 1952 age 19 yrs 10 das

EAHEART, Benjamin T. 17 Dec 1934   Va Pvt 38 Inf 3 Div

BROADUS FAMILY CEMETERY

DIRECTIONS: Route 3 West to Route 601 South. At intersection
of Route 603 there is a house on your left on
Route 601. Behind this house is an old family
cemetery. Very overgrown, no stones were found
but according to Mrs. Day, informant, this cemetery
contains many of her relatives including her parents
aunts, cousins, etc.

Brief genealogy of Mrs Day, informant: She was the daughter of _____
Washington and _____ Woods, her father was the
son of Washington and _____ Broadus whose family
home was at this location. Her husband is
buried at Pilgrim Baptist Church Cemetery. She
recently lost her son who is also at Pilgrim
Baptist Church Cemetery.

SLAVE CEMETERY NEAR BROADUS FARM

DIRECTIONS: Same as for Broadus Family Cemetery, but this
cemetery is in hollow across the road from the
house. Informant: Clyde Johnson said there
were many slaves buried here, without stones,
a very overgrown cemetery.

BROOKS - THURSTON FAMILY CEMETERY

DIRECTIONS: In pines near the Rhoadesville Post Office,
badly overgrown, no stones. Mr Thurston, informant.

BROOKS, Aunts
Cousins
Grandmother [Mr Thurston's mother's mother] Note all of these people
were close kin to Mr Thurston.

BROWN FAMILY CEMETERY

DIRECTIONS: Route 33 West from Gordonsville to Route 678 West.
Just before Route 777 are barns on right. Cemetery
is in field just behind barns. Permission needed.
Plaque on gate: "In memoriam of Mother and Father
Winifred and J. Albert Brown sr."

BROWN, Alverda S. ... see WASHINGTON
    Dennis F. 15 Sept 1864 – 13 Sept 1936
    Edgar 7 Nov 1832 – 23 Feb 1908
    G.J. [large headstone, face down; initials on footstone "G.J.B."]
    George E. 4 Jan 1868 – 27 Aug 1958
    Homassel 1876 – 1924 wife of Rev. J. T. Johnson
    J. Albert 15 July 1830 – 20 Aug 1907 husb of Winifred
    J. Albert 7 Dec 1859 – 24 Jan 1948
    J. B. [large headstone, face down; initials on footstone "J.B.B."]
    Joseph B. 2 Jan 1873 – 21 Apr 1960
    Lou 1862 – 1929 wife of J.E. Gordon
    Oscar P. 1 Jan 1856 – 22 July 1906 "Our Son"
    Parke Farley 1857 – 1925 Sister
    Sarah Ann 1835 – 1920 "Grandmother"
    Thomas H. 17 Mar 1870 – 22 Jan 1956
    Winifred June 1835 – 26 Aug 1913 wife of J. Albert

GORDON, Lou Brown ... see BROWN

JOHNSON, Homassel Brown ... see BROWN

WASHINGTON, Alverda S. 3 July 1862 – 27 Sept 1901 erected by Mother,
    Sarah A. Brown

BICKERS BURIAL PLACE

DIRECTIONS: Route 20 West to Route 600 South. Right on
farm road leading to Lake Orange.

BICKERS, John M. no dates 6th Va Cav Co G CSA

BROWN'S TALL CEDAR FARM CEMETERY

DIRECTIONS: Route 33 West from Barboursville 4 miles. South
on road just before Chestnut Baptist Church for
1.2 miles to end of road for directions. Many
unmarked graves.

MILLER, Leslie Glen 10 June 1882 – 23 May 1918

WOOD, Joseph B. 26 June 1856 – 9 Mar 1883

CAMPBELL FAMILY CEMETERY

DIRECTIONS: Route 3 West to Pilgrim Baptist Church road. Pass
the church and go to the William Keen property.
Cemetery is on left and joins the Reuben Lewis
Farm Cemetery. There are said to be three graves,
however, no markers were found. Informant: Mr.
Jack J. Duval

CAMPBELLTON CEMETERY

DIRECTIONS: Route 33 to last farm road on right before Route
652. Watch or you will need to retrace a very
short distance. Go 0.1 miles to end of road
and lovely old manor house. Cemetery is to
left near modern garage in grove of trees.

CAMPBELL, America W. d. 10 Mar 1862 age 60 years
    Elizabeth Waters d. 23 Feb 1723 age 6 months
    Frederick W. d. 11 Nov 1874 age 64 yrs
    Mildred P. d. 8 Apr 1862 age 69 yrs
    Susan d. 13 Mar 1852 age 87 years
    William [Col.] d. 20 Oct 1825 age 68 years

DULANEY, Catherine H. d. 28 Nov 1874 age 84 years

GIBBS, Elizabeth d. 21 Apr 1852 age 85 years

GRAVES, Emma C. 24 June 1849 - 5 Aug 1959

WELCH, Arria d. 2 Sept 1881 age 84 years

CARTER FAMILY CEMETERY

DIRECTIONS: Route 20 West to Route 522 North for 0.2 miles
to Faith Bible Church on your right. Cemetery is
in pines well behind the church. It has no stones.
Informant:Mr Thornton. These are his maternal
grandparents and other relatives.

CARTER, Aunts
    Cousins
    John [grandfather]
    Uncles

CATTERTON CEMETERY ON BOWMAN PLACE

DIRECTIONS: Route 20 West of Orange to Route 609 West to
Route 610 North for 1.3 miles to end of road.
Park. Cross gate. Follow road until you
pass a barn, an old house foundation, and cross
two runs. Immediately follow wagon road to top
of hill on right. Cemetery is on your left in
deep woods. Permission from house on corner
of Route 609 and Route 610.

CATTERTON, Emma Jane 24 Feb 1851 – 31 Dec 1937 wife of George L.
George L. 11 Mar 1854 – 9 Oct 1927 husb of Emma Jane
Lelia E. ... see POWELL
N.L. 31 Oct 1904 – 3 July 1905 son of Nimrod P. and Lelia E. Catterton
Nimrod P. 6 Aug 1880 – 30 Nov 1951 husb of Lelia E.
S. A. no dates
William W. 11 Feb 1845 – 26 Oct 1924

POWELL, C.G. no dates husb of Susan J., father of Charles L.
Charles LeVert 27 May 1874 – 4 May 1892 son of C.G. and S.J.
Hattie H. 10 Dec 1879 – 1 Mar 1951 wife of Charles F. Sentz
Lelia E. 23 July 1877 – 1 Mar 1941 wife of Nimrod P. Catterton
Susan J. 20 Apr 1847 – 20 Apr 1892 wife of C.G. Powell

SENTZ, Hattie H. ... see POWELL

WALTERS, G.C. 4 Oct 1834 – 10 Dec 1894 father
P.A. 4 Dec 1841 – 16 Feb 1893 wife of G.C.

WILHOIT, Mariah L. 1 Mar 1814 – 27 July 1895

CEMETERY BEACH

DIRECTIONS: Route 20 West to Lake – of – the – Woods entrance
on left. Get directions and permission to enter
from security. Cemetery is on Harrison Circle
on big lake. NOTE: This cemetery has no visible
graves and no stones. The graves were not moved
when the lake was formed. The property was owned
by the Washington – Broadus – Day family at one
time and this may have been a Washington family
cemetery. Information from Lake – of – the –
Woods security.

CLARKE FAMILY CEMETERY

DIRECTIONS: Corner of Route 33 and Route 20 in Barboursville,
              behind the firehouse. Iron fenced, newly painted,
              well cared for cemetery.

CLARKE, Lena Gertrude 21 May 1867 - 22 Jan 1919 wife of Walter K., dau of
              R.D. and Ardema Douglass
     Walter King 5 Mar 1866 - 10 Mar 1922 husb of Lena G.

DOUGLASS, Lena Gertrude ... see CLARKE

COLEMAN CEMETERY

DIRECTIONS: Route 522 South to Route 629 West to Route 649
              South to first farm road on right. Ask Mrs.
              Coleman for permission and directions.

COLEMAN, Edmund Moore 4 Nov 1844 - 5 May 1919
     Eva Taylor 28 Dec 1852 - 12 Mar 1943
     Thomas Lafayett 8 Jan 1880 - 5 June 1880
     Willie Conway 28 Feb 1881 - 12 Apr 1959 never married

TAYLOR, Eva ... see COLEMAN

WOOLFOLK, John Lafayette 23 Sept 1824 - 21 Sept 1890
     Sarah C. d. 1 Aug 1870 age 41 years

COLEMAN - FARISH FAMILY CEMETERY

DIRECTIONS: South on Route 522 to Route 719 East for 0.88 miles
              to farm road just beyond county line. PENNFIELDS
              FARM is in Orange County. Turn left. Cemetery
              is halfway back to house beside road. Ask per-
              mission. House was built in 1804 with addition
              in 1904.

COLEMAN, T.F. 10 Nov 1812 - 6 Aug 1894
     Thos 4 Oct 1853 - 18 Mar 1887

FARISH, Mary E. 18 Jan 1841 - 30 Sept 1906 wife of W.P.T. Farish
     W.P.T. 15 Nov 1838 - 24 Dec 1892

COLEMAN PLACE CEMETERY

DIRECTIONS: From Burr Hill Store on Route 611 go South on
Route 692 for 1.3 miles. Right on Route 640
[dirt road] for 0.2 miles to right fork. Drive
0.2 miles to locked gate. Park. Walk 0.1 miles
to turn in road. Cemetery is on right. There
are five unmarked graves. A cinderblock wall
was being erected when visited. Informant for
names: Clyde Johnson.

COLEMAN, John and wife no dates parents of Clyde and Ellwood Coleman who
live on Route 611

COOPER FAMILY CEMETERY

DIRECTIONS: Route 20 West to Route 650 then almost immediately
take left fork on Route 624 to last curve before
Wyatt - McGehee cemetery. Bear right on farm
road to Cooper cemetery. Cemetery is overgrown
and could not be recorded. NOTE: This is on
the WITT property and is sometimes referred to
as the Witt Cemetery. Informant: Clyde Johnson.

DAVIS FAMILY CEMETERY

DIRECTIONS: Route 33 West to Route 644 North for 2.4 miles
to former "school building" on left. Private
drive, labeled "The Ordinary" just beyond
"school". 0.2 miles downhill cemetery is in
field to your left. It is fenced and in fair
condition. Permission from house at end of
farm road. Eleven unmarked graves.

DAVIS, Virgil R. 20 Apr 1874 - 10 Sept 1919 wife of Thomas J. Davis
Thomas J. Co F 13 Va Inf CSA no dates husb of Virgil R.

DAVIS FAMILY CEMETERY

DIRECTIONS: Route 522 North to Route 663 North to last house
on left before Palmyra Church. Get permission
to visit cemetery which is on hill near old
home. This farm was originally known as MOUNT
Valley. Copied by Ferol Briggs and Mrs. Alfred
Burruss. Furnished by Mr. Briggs.

BAKER, Janet   no dates   wife of James Edward Davis

COLEMAN, George W.   17 Aug 1817 - 11 July 1902   "Our Uncle"

DAVIS, Alice   1871 - 1941
    Catherine E.   20 Aug 1826 - 6 Feb 1903   Erected to the loving memory of my
        sister J.S.S.
    Eliza J.   15 Nov 1812 - 16 Mar 1881   "Our Mother"
    Eugenia Lambert   20 Oct 1915 - 22 Oct 1915   inf dau of T. Russell and Flora
        W. Davis
    _____   18 July 1854 - 16 _____ ____ [not readable] "My sister" A
        footstone marked "F.C.D."
    Fannie C.   17 Dec 1877 - 25 Mar 1906   "Our Daughter"
    Flora Woodward   2 May 1878 - 25 July 1972   wife of Thomas R.
    George Coleman   24 May 1880 - 3 Feb 1902   "Our Dear Boy"
    J.L.   16 Apr 1845 - 18 May 1909
    James Edward   27 Mar 1909 - 29 July 1955   husb of Janet Baker
    James L.   25 Oct 1885 - 7 May 1932
    James M.   25 Nov 1820 - 12 Aug 1872   "Beloved Husband"
    James Taliaferro   18 June 1940 - 11 Apr 1959   son of James E. and Janet B.
    Janet Baker   ...   see   BAKER
    M.C.   19 Dec 1847 - 15 Oct 1920
    Mary   ...   see   ROBERTS
    Russell Conway   17 Feb 1913 - 2 Mar 1928   son of Thomas R. and Flora W.
    Thomas   14 July 1814 - 1874 [not readable, supplied by family member] husb
        of Eliza J.
    Thomas Russell   16 Aug 1873 - 18 June 1951   husb of Flora W.
    Thomas W.   23 Feb 1841 - _____ 1862   son of T. and E.J. Davis. Stone
        fallen in 1974

EUBANK, Mary I. H.   3 Mar 1894 - 28 Aug 1937

HENDERSON, John Uriel   1863 - 1964

MORTON, William   d. 4 Sept 1833   85th year   father, [rest not readable]

NEWMAN, Sarah   ...   see   PEREGORY

PANNILL, David   23 Sept 1812 - 12 May 1882

PEREGORY, Inf   d. 19 Feb 1816   dau of Mrs Sarah Peregory
    Sarah [Mrs.]   d. 19 Feb 1816   dau of Tho. Newman

ROBERTS, James Cameron   28 Apr 1945 - 10 Dec 1961   son of Mary Davis Roberts

SALE, R.C.   6 Nov 1815 - 23 Nov 1886   [stone partially buried]

TIMBERLAKE, Jane   26? May 1811 - 4? May 1854   wife of J.W. Timberlake

WOODWARD, Flora   ...   see   DAVIS

DAWSON CEMETERY NEAR COLVIN PLACE

DIRECTIONS: Route 20 West to Route 609 West to Route 676
             North. Bear right at second farm road to
             Colvin Farm 0.7 miles from turn on to Route 676.
             At the Colvin Farm park, look to your right
             toward the house and barns in valley. The
             Dawson Cemetery was near the site of the present
             tool shed/barn. According to Mr. Colvin only
             one child was ever buried there.

DOUGLASS FAMILY CEMETERY

DIRECTIONS: Route 33 NW about 0.75 miles from Barboursville.
             This property was known as the Artford D. Seeds
             Farm. Contributor unknown. NOTE: Later gener-
             ations spelled the name with one "S" Douglas.

DOUGLASS, Eugenia M. 10 Sept 1847 - 3 June 1922 dau of Francis and Selena
        Eva Margaret 16 Aug 1859 - 23 Oct 1862 grand-daughter of Francis E. and
                 Selena M. Douglass
        Francis E. 1 Feb 1822 - 12 May 1884 husb of Selena M.
        Selena M. 18 Oct 1826 - 27 Feb 1894 wife of Francis E.

SEEDS, Mary Hildreth 10 Nov 1911 - 20 Mar 1925 great-grand-daughter of
                 Francis E. and Selena M. Douglass
        Mary M. 17 May 1879 - 12 Feb 1902 grand-daughter of Francis E. and
                 Selena M. Douglass
        Robert Carrol 25 May 1915 - 20 Jan 1937 great-grand-son of Francis E.
                 and Selena M. Douglass [no tombstone]

DUVAL FAMILY CEMETERY

DIRECTIONS: Route 3 West to entrance of Lake - of - the -
             Woods on East side of Route 3. There are two
             houses. Beyond the house on the left side of
             the road are three unmarked graves. These are
             the graves of Mr. Duval's parents and his aunt.
             He did not recall the dates. Informant: Mr.
             Jack J. Duval.

EDGEMONT CEMETERY

DIRECTIONS: Route 3 West to Lake-of-the-Woods entrance on left. Get permission and directions from security to find this cemetery which contains five native stones and no inscriptions. It is located on Lakeview drive between the two outlets to Edgemont Circle.

ELMERS FARM CEMETERY

DIRECTIONS: Route 20 West to Route 611 South to Route 621 West to Route 692 South to Route 651 West to Route 687 South for 1.5 miles to Cemetery on right. 9 native stones. No inscriptions. Very well maintained.

FAULCONER FAMILY CEMETERY

DIRECTIONS: From Orange Route 615 North to Route 627 East to Route 697 North for 1.8 miles to end of Road. Mr. Coleman at Moormont Orchards was our informant and will give permission to visit. NOTE: No tombstones were found, but there were four natural stones.

CEMETERY ON TOM FELDMAN PLACE

DIRECTIONS: Route 20 East from Orange to Route 600 South to Route 714 East. Cross ford and continue to locked gate. Through gate to house at top of hill. Be certain you lock gate so that cattle are safe. Mr or Mrs Tom Feldman will take you to the cemetery. NOTE: No stones were found, but evidence of several sunken graves and of native stone markers. Mrs. Feldman did not know the identity of the cemetery.

GERMANNA CEMETERY

DIRECTIONS: Route 3 West to Germanna Memorial Park. Take
left road into park. Bear left for 0.05 miles
to left fork. Continue for 50 yards. Cemetery
is on left covered with myrtle or periwinkle.
NOTE: There are additional unmarked graves.

URQUHART, Finnelia d. 23 May 1816 50th year of her life. wife of Charles
Urquhart

GORDON HOUSE CEMETERY AT GERMANNA

DIRECTIONS: None given. Contributed by Charles Duval

BILLINGSLEY, Bettie S. 1 Sept 1835 - 4 Oct 1880 wife of John D.
John Dabney 8 Oct 1833 - 9 Mar 1924 husb of Bettie S.
John P. 21 Mar 1863 - 12 Apr 1888

GORDON, John Addison 13 Nov 1812 - 31 Mar 1883

GRAVE AT FIVE FORKS

DIRECTIONS: Route 3 West to Pilgrim Baptist Church road.
Continue past church and past Reuben Lewis
Farm cemetery and past Campbell cemetery to
"U" turn in road, an area known as "Five Forks"
where there is one grave on left side of road,
unmarked. Informant: Mr Jack J. Duval

GRAVES FAMILY CEMETERY

DIRECTIONS: Route 33 West from Gordonsville to Route 652
North for 1.5 miles to end of road. Cemetery is
on left behind house. Ask permission.

DARGAN, Ethel Forester 19 July 1882 - 23 Oct 1901 dau of Dr. Edwin Charles
and Lucy A. Dargan
John Herbert 15 Dec 1880 - 20 Dec 1880 son of E.C. and Lucy A. Dargan
Lucy Augusta 9 Apr 1851 - 30 Oct 1940 widow of Dr. Edwin Charles Dargan,
mother of Ethel Forrester Dargan and John Herbert
Dargan

GRAVES, Charles Hubert 25 Sept 1863 - 4 July 1866 son of Capt W.C. and
Martha Ann
Martha Ann Hiden 12 Jan 1829 - 17 Jan 1922 wife of Capt Wm C., mother
of Lucy Augusta Graves Dargan
William Crittenden [Capt.] 13 Oct 1828 - 10 May 1912 CSA husb of Martha
Ann Hiden, father of Lucy Augusta Graves Dargan
William Preston 25 Feb 1857 - 23 Mar 1890 born in Orange, died in Augusta,
Georgia; son of Capt W.C. and Martha A. Graves

HIDEN, Martha Ann ... see GRAVES

GREENFIELDS CEMETERY

DIRECTIONS: On unmarked road in Orange one block East of
Route 2001 in new Greenfields Subdivision.
Cemetery is walled and behind original farmhouse.

HOWARD, Charles P. 25 Nov 1765 - 20 Mar 1856 born in Philadelphia, died at
his late residence this county
Jane Taylor ... see TAYLOR

TAYLOR, E. Moore 22 Dec 1728 - 19 Sept 181_
Erasmus 5 Sept 1715 - 18 Dec 1794
J.M. [footstone only "JMT"]
Jane 2 Mar 1766 - 13 Jan 1849 beloved wife of Charles P. Howard

HALSEY FAMILY CEMETERY AT LESSLAND

DIRECTIONS: North on Route 522 to last left before river.
West on Route 636 for 0.2 miles to Route 626
South for 0.1 miles. Watch for large red brick
house with white pillars on right. Name on mail
box is "Bennett", but this is the old Halsey
homestead and Mrs. Bennett was a Halsey. She
first married a "Spotswood" second Mr Bennett.
She has many photographs and a family Bible and
knows a great deal about the Halsey family.

DICKENSON, Fannie Morton Halsey ... see HALSEY

HALSEY, Fannie D. 6 Jan 1884 - 4 Dec 1963 wife of Franklin S., dau of James
and Fannie Halsey Dickinson
Fannie Morton 1848 - 1936 wife of James Dickenson, mother of Fannie D.
Halsey
Franklin Stearns 29 Oct 1882 - 16 Sept 1920 husb of Fannie D.
Irena Louisa 16 Sept 1907 - 16 Nov 1908 dau of F.S. and F.D. Halsey
James b and d 1916 son of F.S. and F.D. Halsey

HAYDEN FAMILY CEMETERY

DIRECTIONS: Route 20 West to Route 611 South to Route 604
              South to Route 608 South. At county line on
              left side of road is the Joe Hayden Family
              Cemetery. No markers except native stones. In-
              formant: Walt Sullivan.

HAYDEN, Joe   no dates

THE HEDRICK HOUSE CEMETERY

DIRECTIONS: Not given. This cemetery is on the old WHEELER
              place. It can be reached only with four wheel
              drive vehicle. Probably no stones remain. Was
              not visited. Informant: Clyde Johnson.

HEFLIN FAMILY GRAVEYARD

DIRECTIONS: Route 3 West to Route 601 Southeast. At fork,
              bear right on Route 603 for 4.2 miles. Turn
              right to road marked "Meadow Trail Ride". Park.
              At bottom of ravine formed by two roads is a small
              graveyard with natural stones. It is thought to
              be a HEFLIN family graveyard as their house once
              stood nearby.

HERNDON FAMILY CEMETERY

DIRECTIONS: Route 20 West to Route 623 North for 1.0 miles to
              end of road. Turn left down overgrown farm road
              to small house on left. Mr. Woodrow Apperson
              [b. 1917] will lead you to this cemetery and the
              APPERSON family cemetery, both in dense under-
              brush and within 0.3 miles of the house.

APPERSON, Lucy ... see HERNDON

HERNDON, David C. no dates Co 28 Va Inf CSA, grandfather of informant,
                            husb of Lucy Apperson
         Hannah no stone, aunt of informant
         Lucy no stone, dau of David C. and Lucy, aunt of informant
         Lucy Apperson no stone wife of David C., grandmother of informant.

HUGHES FAMILY CEMETERY

DIRECTIONS: Route 20 West to Route 650 South to Route 624
South to farm road on left just before Mt Olive
Church. Road has "Chewnings Farm" on mail box.
East on farm road for 0.2 miles to house and
cemetery on right. There may be as many as forty
unmarked graves.

HERNDON, Mary Ann ... see HUGHES

HUGHES, Mary Ann Herndon 7 May 1830 – 3 Jan 1904 wife
   Virginia Louise 19 Dec 1916 – 14 Oct 1918 [Family tradition says that the
child is said to have died from flu, but more immediately
because the doctor left an overdose of medication. When
he realized and returned to the house to stop the family
from giving it to the child, she was already dead.]
   Wyatte Jefferson 26 May 1825 – 1 Jan 1895 husband

JONES, Mary Ann d. 21 Aug 1900
   Wm A. 12 Sept 1825 – 13 May 1904 husband

INDIAN MOUND ON COLVIN PLACE

DIRECTIONS: Route 20 West to Route 609 West to Route 676
North. Bear right at second farm road to
Colvin Farm 0.7 miles from turn on Route 676.
At Colvin Farm, park. Look beyond the YOWELL –
COLLINS Cemetery for about 200 yards to tallest
tree. That is the Indian mound. Many artifacts
and evidence of burials have been found here.

JACKSON CEMETERY

DIRECTIONS: Route 522 South from Route 20 to Route 629.
Cemetery is in field to Southwest of corners.
There are possibly four or five additional graves.

JACKSON, Jane G. 3 Nov 1848 – 18 Apr 1928 wife of Joe

JACKSON CEMETERY

DIRECTIONS: Route 522 South to Route 629 West to first drive
beyond Route 669. Drive is on left. Go 0.05 miles
to cemetery in field on right. Well fenced. This
is Mrs. Lizzie Rider's farm.

BROWN, Mary J. 19 July 1850 - 11 May 1899

DANIEL, J.M. d. 18 Dec 1902 age 79 years 8 months
    Mildred A. 27 Feb 1831 - 22 Feb 1907 "Our Mother"

JACKSON, Joseph S. [Elder] 29 Aug 1805 - 6 July 1854 husb of Mary
        "Dear as thou wert and Justly dear
        We will not weep for thee
        One thought shall check startling tear
        It is that thou art free
        and thus shall faith's consoling power
        the tears of love restrain
        O who that saw thy parting hour
        could wish thee here again
        Triumphant in thy closing eye
        the hope of glory show
        Joy breathed in thy expiring sigh
        to think the race was run.
        The passing spirit gently fled
        sustained by Grace Devine
        O may such Grace on us be shed
        and make our end like thine."

    Mary 18 May 1808 - 10 Feb 1882 wife of Elder Joseph S. Jackson

JERDONE CEMETERY AT BLOOMSBURY

DIRECTIONS: Route 20 South of airport. There is a historical
marker [highway sign] about Bloomsbury. Get permission to enter road.

CAMPER, Infant no dates

JERDONE, Catherine Robinson 1850 - 1926
    Eliza Mayo 1810 - 1884
    Francis III 1802 - 1874
    Frank 1846 - 1923
    Infant no dates
    John 1839 - 1889
    Lillie Robinson 1853 - 1886
    Walter Peyton 1836 - 1864
    William M. 1 May 1842 - 1 June 1872

MAYO, Eliza ... see JERDONE

ROBINSON, Catherine ... see JERDONE
    Lillie ... see JERDONE
    Lucy May 1847 - 1931

WATKINS, Anne d. 1861
    Edward d. 1858

JOHNSON FAMILY CEMETERY

DIRECTIONS: Route 20 West to Route 611 North to Mt. Pisgah
Church corners. South on Route 672 for 0.1 miles.
Through gate for 0.2 miles to cemetery. This is
called "Campbell's Grounds". Permission at Burr
Hill Store. NOTE: There are at least 8 unmarked
graves.

HUME, Nora L. Johnson 8 Oct 1906 - 22 Dec 1934

JOHNSON, Ella 11 July 1869 - 5 Feb 1910
    G.S. 17 May 1818 - 3 June 1907
    James I. 18 Sept 1920 - 8 Dec 1943 Penn Pfc 142 Inf WW II
    Mary Elizabeth 18 May 1840 - 4 May 1909
    Nora L. ... see HUME
    Robert F. 26 Mar 1866 - 13 Oct 1944
    William M. 9 Jan 1838 - 18 Dec 1917

JONES FAMILY CEMETERY

DIRECTIONS: Route 20 North from Barboursville to Route 745
West for 0.2 miles to cemetery on left. Permission
at next house beyond cemetery. Informant: Mrs.
Nelson Jones.

BEASLEY, Juanita Jones d. c. 1943 age "in 40's" dau of Nelson Jones

JONES, Earl Ray d. 15 Nov 1969 age 30 years 4 months 5 days son of Nelson
    Juanita ... see BEASLEY
    Nelson 2 June 1894 - 4 Apr 1963 Va Pvt USA WW II

JONES FAMILY CEMETERY

DIRECTIONS: Route 20 West to Route 611 North to Route 620
[first entrance] North to Route 681 East to end
of road. This is an old JONES cemetery on what is
known as the HANSBOROUGH place. Informant:
Clyde Johnson. No stones.

KENNEDY - HUME FAMILY CEMETERY AT ELMWOOD

DIRECTIONS: From Orange North on Route 615 for 1.0 miles
to Elmwood on left. Cemetery is walled, has a
stile [built in 1923 by Johnson Butler] and is
extremely well kept.

BLAIR, Bessie ... see SISSON

GRADY, Alice ... see KENNEDY

HUME, Albert W. 1858 - 1908

HUME and KENNEDY Negro Servants "In Memory of the Faithful Negro Servants
of the Hume and Kennedy Families"

HUME, Carrie Lee 26 Mar 1854 - 3 Sept 1924
 Charles W. 18 May 1818 - 19 Oct 1892 husb of Louise V.S.
 David 8 Mar 1808 - 28 Feb 1857 husb of Frances E.
 Fanny L. 1825 - 1908
 Frances E. d. Mar 1846 [a Sunday, date missing, stone broken] age 33 years
        2 months 26 days wife of David
 Francis 22 May 1834 - 1 Nov 1837
 Louisa V. S. 2 Aug 1830 - 22 Sept 1866 wife of Charles W. Hume
 Mary 8 May 1830 - 2 Jan 1835 dau of David and Frances
 Mary E. 1819 - 1900
 Sarah Ann 1861 - 1884
 W. W. [Dr.] 9 May 1856 - 28 Aug 1922
 William Waller 1781 - 1870

KENNEDY, Albert 1792 - 1864
 Alice Grady 4 May 1871 - 5 Jan 1935
 Barbara A. 1818 - 1843
 Caroline E. 1822 - 1842
 Dora ... see SISSON
 Edgar Sumter 3 Dec 1861 - 21 Aug 1953
 Eliza Peyton 1831 - 1853
 Ellen M. 1827 - 1910 mother, wife of Jas F.H.
 Ida Smith 1857 - 1858
 Jas F.H. 1827 - 1908 father, husb of Ellen M.
 Lucy A. 1820 - 1821
 Matilda 1797 - 1862
 Nellie ... see TATUM

PEYTON, Eliza ... see KENNEDY

SISSON, Bessie Blair 1884 - 1886 same stone as James Russell Sisson
 Dora Kennedy 1855 - 1943 mother
 Edgar S. 1889 - 1890 same stone as Oscar L.
 James Russell 1883 - 1886 same stone as Bessie Blair
 John Row 1857 - 1916 father
 Oscar L. 1889 - 1889 same stone as Edgar S.

SMITH, Ida ... see KENNEDY

TATUM, Nellie Kennedy 29 Dec 1886 - 10 Nov 1943 mother

KESTNER'S FAMILY CEMETERY

DIRECTIONS: Route 20 West to Route 692 South. Just beyond
             Route 606 is a house on right. On the far side
             of the field a single infant grave was removed
             and placed in another cemetery in 1975.

LACEY FARM CEMETERY

DIRECTIONS: Route 20 West from Wilderness Corner to the first
             farm road on left. Get permission from ranger at
             Chancellor Battlefield Exhibit. Area is park
             property and is closed to the public.

JACKSON, Stonewall's Arm   amputated 3 May 1863. [Note: Jackson was re-
             moved to Guinea where he died on 10 May 1863]

LAMB CEMETERY

DIRECTIONS: From county line on 657 go 1.0 miles Southeast to
             first brick house on right. LAMB is name on
             mail box. Behind the house about 50 yards is a
             small fenced cemetery with native stones, no
             inscriptions. Surname for cemetery was not
             available.

DAVID LEWIS FAMILY CEMETERY

DIRECTIONS: Route 20 East from Route 33 at Barboursville for
             0.1 miles North of North end of Route 738. Sign
             "Maple Hill" W.R.Brock. This drive goes over part
             of the cemetery. There are no inscribed markers,
             but several depressions marked by native stones.
             Gentleman who lives in house to left said last
             burial was at least twenty years ago. It is re-
             corded here.

LEWIS, David buried c. 1958   also many of his family members

REUBEN LEWIS FARM CEMETERY

DIRECTIONS: Route 3 West for 1.4 miles beyond Route 20 to
Pilgrim Baptist Church road. Turn right. Pass
church. Go 0.1 miles to Wm Keen property. The
cemetery lies on a line S17° 16' 07" E approximately 500' to left of the road. House and dug
well remains can be seen. There are five native
stones and property belonged to Reuben Lewis for
many years.

LOYD FAMILY CEMETERY

DIRECTIONS: Route 33 West to Route 644. Right on Route 644 to
Route 655 right to Route 657 to end of road. Park
and walk 100 yards on old road to open field.
Then walk 100 yards across open field toward old
pear tree. Cemetery is in pine woods just beyond
the tree at far side of field.

HALL, Florence Virginia Loyd   24 Jan 1890 - 3 Nov 1933

LOYD, Florence Virginia   ...   see   HALL

LUCAS FARM CEMETERY

DIRECTIONS: Standing in front of the Herman May home on Route
657 just across the Greene County Line, he pointed
to the Northeast and said, "There's a cemetery on
the Lucas place you could reach only by helicopter
and maybe not then." The information below is
recorded from his memory of three funerals he
attended.

COLVIN, Julia   no dates   wife of Melvin
    Melvin   no dates   husb of Julia [2 July 1861 - 15 Feb 1934   son of Matthew
                           and Mary Lillard Colvin (mortician's record)]
HOFFMAN, _____

LUCAS - TURNER FAMILY CEMETERY

DIRECTIONS: From Mine Run South on Route 608 for 1.7 miles.
Cemetery is on right in field across from THOMAS
Farm. No stones. Recalled from memory by Mrs.
Ethel Wallace Wheeler who owns house next door.

LUCAS, Ernest c. 1950 husb of Julie
   Julie c. 1950 wife of Ernest

TURNER, Arthur   husb of "Aunt Sally"
   Sally around 1935 wife of Arthur

LUMSDEN FAMILY CEMETERY

DIRECTIONS: Route 522 South to Route 629 East to Route 651
0.3 miles beyond Route 624. Take road on your
right that is nearer Route 624. 1.2 miles to end
of road. Cemetery is in field directly ahead.
NOTE: There are seven natural stone markers.

CHEWNING, Allie 19 Mar 1877 - 30 May 1923

LUMSDEN, Charlie L. 8 Apr 1845 - 12 May 1922 husb of Mary L.
   E. Frank 5 Mar 1873 - 7 Nov 1928
   Henry Clay no dates Crenshaw's Co Va Art CSA
   Inez I. 5 Jan 1880 - 13 Nov 1940
   John R. 27 July 1871 - 19 Nov 1872
   Matilda H. 7 Apr 1840 - 13 Apr 1922
   Mary L. 25 June 1857 - 5 July 1922 wife of Charlie
   Vernon O. 4 Sept 1874 - 22 Apr 1927

MACDONALD CEMETERY AT EVERDURE

DIRECTIONS: Route 615 North from Orange to Route 627. Everdure is well marked and is the last farm road to
the left before Route 697. NOTE: The stones
are unique. Large field stones were used for
the monuments with lovely hand made metal plaques.
The plaques were stamped with the branding irons
used on the cattle. They are simple and attractive.
Also: Avery, son of Angus Snead Macdonald, died
in an airplane accident and was cremated. His
ashes were sprinkled over Lake Michigan. The
stone and plaque are a suitable memorial to him.
Informant: Mrs Amy B. Macdonald.

MACDONALD, Angus Avery 18 Sept 1918 - 4 Aug 1970 see note above
   Angus Snead 7 Nov 1888 - 2 Feb 1961 husb of Amy B. Macdonald, father
of Angus Avery Macdonald

PRESIDENT MADISON CEMETERY

DIRECTIONS: Route 20 West of Orange. Pass Montpelier Station
              left on next road which is Route 639. Road is
              marked to Cemetery. Cemetery is maintained by
              DAR.

CARSON, Frank d. Feb 1881 age 62 years Native of Lislee, Ireland d. at
             Montpelier

CONWAY, Lucy H. Macon ... see MACON
        Reuben 11 Mar 1788 - 3 Jan 1838

LEE, Ambrose Madison 17 Feb 1832 - 26 Mar 1838 "My Son"
     John Wills 27 Mar 1836 - 16 Feb 1837
     Lucy C. 16 Mar 1834 - 26 Aug 1855 "My Sister"
     Mary W. 8 Sept 1806 - 29 Mar 1836 married 21 Mar 1826 "My Wife"

MACON, J. Madison 3 July 1791 - 8 Feb 1877
       Lucetta T. Newman ... see NEWMAN
       Lucy H. 21 Feb 1794 - 13 May 1871 wife of Reuben Conway
       Sarah G. 17 May 1761 - 17 Oct 1848 wife of Thomas, dau of James Madison sr
       Thomas 11 June 1765 - 26 Feb 1838

MADISON, Alfred 10 Aug 1861 - 12 May 1880
         Ambrose 12 Mar 1796 - 26 Dec 1855
         Ambrose G. d. 28 Feb 1928 age 81 yrs son of Dr. James and Lucy Hiden
              Madison
         Dolley Payne 20 May 1768 - 6 July 1849 wife of James Madison
         Fannie W. 9 Apr 1842 - 28 Oct 1899 wife of Jas A. Madison
         James [President's tomb has only surname and dates on large obelisk] 16 Mar
              1751 - 28 June 1836
         James 26 Nov 1855 - 16 Feb 1916
         James A. [Dr.] 14 July 1828 - 28 June 1901
         Letitia R. L. 20 June 1829 - 2 Jan 1857 consort of Dr. R.L. Madison
         Lucy M. 24 June 1830 - 27 July 1886 "Our Mother"
         Susan Daniel 1854 - 1938 dau of Dr. James A. and Lucy Maria Madison

MARYE, Mary F. 12 Apr 1822 - 13 Nov 1856 "The subject of this memorial was
                possessed of an intelligent mind, and an eminentaly (sic)
                amiable and unselfish disposition. In the tender re-
                lationship of wife and mother, she faithfully and af-
                fectionately discharged the duties which devolved upon
                her in all her intercourse displayed the uncomplaining
                excellence of charm and the memory of her values will
                long survive in the bereaved hearts of her family and
                the kind regard of all who knew her."

NEWMAN, Lucetta T. 9 Jan 1799 - 1 Jan 1878 wife of J. Madison Macon

PAYNE, Dolley ... see MADISON

ROSS, Nellie 1 Aug 1875 - 12 Apr 1893 "My Sister" dau of John and Mary E.
      Willis

WILLIS, Claudia 14 Feb 1869 - 14 Mar 1869 dau of Lucie S. and John Willis
        Fannie 27 July 1820 - 12 Aug 1859 wife of John Willis married 14 Aug 1839

WILLIS, John [Dr.] 24 Oct 1774 - 1 Apr 1811 born Whitehall, Glouster, died
                                           at Woodley, Orange
   John 8 Jan 1810 - 9 Dec 1885
   Lucie S. 21 Dec 1844 - 17 Feb 1869 married 21 June 1866 wife of John Willis
   Lucy d. 16 Feb 18_8 [either 1868 or 1888] age 47 wife of John Willis
   Mary ?[5 Nov] 1844 - Aug 1859 dau of John and Fannie Lee Willis
   Nellie ... see ROSS

MANUAL LEVEL FARM
[WHITELAW - SIMS - MASON FAMILY CEMETERY]

DIRECTIONS: Route 33 West to Route 607 South. Make an im-
             mediate right into farm road leadind to Manual
             Level. Estate now owned by Rene C. and Jeannine
             M. DesJardins. NOTE: Other graves both with and
             without decipherable markers. Mrs. Edith Sims
             of Barboursville has a complete plot of cemetery.

DAVIS, Mary ... see SIMS

HARLOW, Dan H. 9 Sept 1894 - 4 Apr 1923

MASON, Wyle Charles [M.D.] 30 July 1891 - 10 Aug 1967 Lt [MC] USN WW I

NORQUIST, Edith ... see SIMS

SIMS, Anna Kelly 30 Apr 1907 - 10 Feb 1909
   Children, [two] no dates
   David 9 Apr 1825 age 36 years husb of Mary Davis
   Edith Norquist d. 10 Mar 1954 age 75 years
   Mary Davis [dates can not be read] wife of David, dau of Isaac Davis
   Robert Angus 29 Jan 1911 - 25 Nov 1964 Mason

MANUAL LEVEL SLAVE CEMETERY

DIRECTIONS: Same as above, but go to house for permission
             and further directions. NOTE: This cemetery
             occupies between one and two acres and contains
             more than 100 sunken graves, some with native
             stone markers, none with identification or in-
             scriptions of any sort.

             The house was built in 1817 so many graves may
             be as old as that and certainly the cemetery was
             in use before 1865.

MARSHALL FAMILY CEMETERY

DIRECTIONS: Route 15 North from Orange to last house on
right before river. There is a cattle guard
and house is white. Ask permission at the
farm formerly called "The Glebe"   as well as
at this home. Cemetery is in field on edge of
woods.

MARSHALL, Elizabeth J. 25 Oct 1822 – 24 July 1903 wife of John W.
John W. 13 Nov 1824 – 11 Feb 1899 husb of Elizabeth J.

B.J. Marshall's BISMARK [Elizabeth J.'s dog. Tombstone has a statue
of a dog on top of it and grave is small]

MASSEY FAMILY CEMETERY

DIRECTIONS: From Mine Run South on Route 608 for 1.7 miles to
THOMAS FARM on left. Cemetery is near barns, is
fenced and in good repair.

FAULCONER, Benjamin 1822 – 1874 husb of Mary Anne Massey
Mary Anne Massey 1820 – 1899 wife of Benjamin Faulconer

HARIS, B.H. native stone, very difficult to read

LEE, Eliza Massey 6 May 1827 – 17 May 1863 wife of Lafayett Lee
Lafayett no dates husb of Eliza Massey

MASSEY, Asa J. Co E 9 Va Cav CSA husb of Sally Ann
Coosa Roberta 20 Feb 1862 – 30 Mar 1930
Eliza ... see LEE
John Hansford 14 July 1883 – 25 Oct 1962
Mary Anne ... see FAULCONER
Oscar Gillispie 1 Mar 1858 – 2 Feb 1934
Sally Ann 23 Sept 1824 – 12 Mar 1902 wife of Asa J. Massey

MODENA FAMILY CEMETERY

DIRECTIONS: Route 20 West to Route 231 South to Route 655.
Ask permission and directions from house on
Southeast corner. Fenced, overgrown.

BRADSHAW, Wilmer Cowan 24 May 1891 – 12 Oct 1891 son of W. J. and Nannie

MODENA, Mrs Alice d. 4 Apr _____ age 84 years

MODENA, Charles H. d. 13 Dec 1911 in his 40th year husb of B. S. Modena,
                father of infant son
    Infant 4 Feb 1900 - 16 Mar 1900 son of C.H. and B.S. Modena
    James William 8 Sept 1808 - 8 July 1890 son of B.J. and Bettie Modena

MONTEBELLO CEMETERY
[CAVE FAMILY CEMETERY]

> DIRECTIONS: From Orange North on Route 15 to Route 632 East
>   0.6 miles beyond RR overpass, then left on first
>   farm road. The pillars are marked "Montebello,
>   1728" and farm has been in Cave family for
>   several generations. Permission at the house
>   and directions from Mrs. Gray Dunnington.

CAVE, Agnes Macon 1855 - 1856 [On separate stone "Agnes, dau of F.H. and
                E.A. Cave 13 Dec 1855 - 12 Aug 1856"]
    Ann Maria 1823 - 1859 [On separate stone "Ann M. Cave Our Sister 13 Aug
                1823 - 30 May 1959"]
    Benjamin I [first] 1680 - 1762 husb of Hannah Bledsoe
    Benjamin II [second] 20 Dec 1735 - Mar 1832
    Eliz Belfield 19 Mar 1738 - Dec 1810
    Elizabeth Belfield June 1845 - 16 Apr 1900
    Elizabeth Branch 1812 - 1884
    Isabella deLacy 1813 - 23 May 1885   [see also GRAY]
    Lucy Cornelia 1822 - 1849 [On separate stone "L. Cornelia Cave Sister
                6 July 1822 - 2 July 1849"]
    Lucy D. b & d 1809
    Mary Frances 1818 - 1862
    Richard 8 Aug 1780 - 6 Apr 1863 husb of Maria father of Georgianna
    Thomas B. b & d 1809
    William Porter 13 Aug 1810 - 22 Oct 1890

deLACY, Isabella ... see CAVE

GRAY, Isabella deLacy Cave Thompson 24 Nov 1871 - 2 May 1962
    Leslie Belfield 6 Oct 1904 - 27 Mar 1947
    Leslie H. 4 Feb 1850 - 16 Apr 1934

JOHNSON, Georgiana Cave 1813 - 1880 [On separate stone "16 Dec 1813 -
                4 Dec 1880 wife of Dr Peter T. Johnson, dau of
                Richard and Maria Cave."]

THOMPSON, Isabella deL C. ... see GRAY
    Maria Cornelia Cave 4 July 1842 - 9 Apr 1903
    William Cave 1869 - 1971

MOORE CEMETERY AT EVERDURE

DIRECTIONS: Route 522 North to Route 701 West to Route 617/627
to next farm road beyond Route 697 on right. Farm
is clearly marked "EVERDURE" Owner: Mrs Amy B.
Macdonald. NOTE: Property was purchased by
Angus Snead Macdonald and his wife, Amy B. Macdonald in June 1937. At that time there were seven
graves. While they were away the following
January [1938] an eighth and final burial took
place. In July of 1958 a single stone was erected
containing six names and initialed footstones.
The other two graves remain unmarked. No dates
were given.

MOORE, Charles H. footstone, no dates
Charles W. no dates, footstone
Edgar no dates, footstone [d. 12 Aug 1929 age 54 son of Wm & Va. Bell Moore
Eleanor P. no dates, footstone   mortician's log]
Mollie V. no dates, footstone
Virginia B. no dates, footstone

MORRIS FAMILY CEMETERY

DIRECTIONS: Route 20 West to Route 611 North to fork in road
just at Zoar Baptist Church. Take Right fork
Route 603 to HOLMES mailbox. There is an unmarked cemetery in the yard where Mrs. Robert
Rhoades great-grandparents are buried.

MORRIS, Great Grandfather no dates great-grandfather of Mrs. Robert Rhoades
who was a Tinder. This was her father's grandfather.
Her father's mother was also a Morris.
Great Grandmother see above

MORTON FAMILY CEMETERY
[OAK GREEN FARM #1]

DIRECTIONS: Route 522 North to Route 663 0.8 miles Northeast
to Oak Green Farm sign. Right for 0.3 miles to
cemetery just beyond barns and cinder block house.
Cemetery has electric fence. Get permission to
visit. Mrs Wallace Jones says there were other
graves when she used to walk there in the 1930's .

MORTON, William d. 4 Sept 1835 age 85 years large obelisk monument.

MT GLEN FARM CEMETERY

DIRECTIONS: From Orange Route 615 North for 3.1 miles past
Route 700 to next long blacktop road on right.
House is painted white brick, sits well back off
road. Cemetery is 0.5 miles across fields to
property line on East and is in wooded area. This
cemetery is on the adjacent farm, but is reach
best from Mt. Glen. Specific directions at house.

MALLORY, David G. no dates Co A 13 Va Inf CSA

MUNDY FAMILY CEMETERY

DIRECTIONS: From Orange North on Route 15 to Route 632 East
0.6 miles beyond RR overpass then right on farm
road at end of State Maintenance sign [across
from Montebello]. Fenced, very well kept. Only
marker is CSA cross. Informant: Mrs Philip
Mundy. Starred information from Family Bible.

*GOODWIN, Charles Edward b. 5 Nov 1829 husb of Sarah Margaret Mason,
father of Mary Goodwin Mundy [buried elsewhere]
  Mary ... see MUNDY
  * Sarah Margaret Mason b. 25 Aug 1835 wife of Charles Edward, mother of
Mary Goodwin Mundy [buried elsewhere]

LANCASTER, Mrs. _____ no stone , no dates mother of first two wives of
Burrus Mundy

MASON, Sarah Margaret ... see GOODWIN

MUNDY, Burrus d. 29 May 1902 age 72 years CSA three wives, sixteen children
m. 1] a Lancaster, buried elsewhere
2] sister of #1 buried here
3] Mary Goodwin buried in Graham
  _____Lancaster no stone no dates second wife of Burrus buried here
  * Mary Goodwin 3rd wife of Burrus Mundy, dau of Sarah Margaret Mason
and Charles Edward Goodwin. Buried at Graham.

NOTE: Family Bible has been copied by Carey Johnson, son of Maggie French
Johnson, grandson of Burrus Mundy. Carey Johnson
resides in Ellicot City, Maryland [1978]

MURPHY - WORMLEY FAMILY CEMETERY

DIRECTIONS: South on Route 522 to Route 719 [Za Corners]
Left on Route 719 for 0.1 miles to cemetery
on left. There are six native stone markers
and several unmarked graves as well.

MURPHY, Myrtle Shirley 20 May 1893 - 15 Feb 1973

WORMLEY, Charles d. 31 Aug 1962 age 62

NEWMAN FAMILY CEMETERY

DIRECTIONS: Route 20 West to 1.5 miles beyond the airport.
Owner: Huey Richards will give permission to
enter nicely fenced cemetery in field on right.

DONAHUE, Genevieve ... see NEWMAN

HARRIS, Imogene ... see NEWMAN

LARMAND, Maria F. 18 Nov 1818 - 6 May 1866 "Our Mother"

NEWMAN, Cora A. 18 July 1864 - 23 Sept 1902 wife of William Q. Newman
Genevieve Donahue 1890 - 1915
Imogene Harris 1881 - 1918
John R. 1822 - 1892
Lucy d. 27 Oct 1848 in her 60th year
Margaret Rogers 1833 - 1891
William 10 June 1777 - 9 Oct 1857
William Q. 6 Sept 1860 - 18 Sept 1935 husb of Cora A.

ROGERS, Margaret ... see NEWMAN

OCTAGONIA GRANT SLAVE CEMETERY

DIRECTIONS: Route 20 West to Route 609 West for 2.5 miles
to Route 644 South for 1.0 mile. Long drive on
left leads to house for permission and further
directions. The slave cemetery lies between the
drive and Beaver Run. No stones remain, no
records of the names.

PANNILL CEMETERY

DIRECTIONS: From True Blue Corners East on Route 611 to first
road on right, Route 684, which is State maintained
for 0.5 miles. There is a locked gate at the end
of the road. It was open during the haying season.
The road continues for 0.1 miles and turns left
for another 0.6 miles to another locked gate.
Beyond gate road turns right to a nicely fenced
and well maintained cemetery before barns or house.

PANNILL, Alice S. 1856 - 1942
    Annie P. 1859 - 1935
    Blanche 1881 - 1912
    Dannie F. 1878 - 1926
    Delia C. 1892 - 1911
    George M. b & d 1894
    G. Morton 1854 - 1941
    Harry Lee 1892 - 1896
    Infant no dates child of Mr and Mrs J.W. Pannill
    Lee 1859 - 1913
    Mattie Porter 1830 - 1972
    Phillip P. 22 Oct 1883 - 1 May 1939
    Phillip Payne 1827 - 1898
    Phillipp Payne 1860 - 1892
    Robert Dandridge 1835 - 1894

PORTER, John A. 12 Nov 1798 - 4 Feb 1864 husb of Mary C. "Our Father"
    Mary C. 15 Sept 1804 - 7 Apr 1857 wife of John A. "Our Mother"
    Mattie ... see PANNILL

PANNILL CEMETERY

DIRECTIONS: From True Blue Corners South on Route 663 to first
gate on right. Recorded during haying as entire
field was planted. Drive 0.4 miles through field
to nicely fenced, but overgrown cemetery with
"Pannill" on gate.

ELIASON, William P. 26 Jan 1807 - Nov 1870

PANNILL, Fannie B. Williams ... see WILLIAMS
    Fannie Bruce 1853 - 1937

WILLIAMS, Fannie B. 1819 - 1909 wife of Joseph B. Pannill

PANNILL SLAVE CEMETERY

DIRECTIONS: As you leave the last cemetery, stop just before
                the gate and look backward to a fencerow on your
                left. There is a break in the fencerow and an
                old Dogwood tree. Several natural stones and
                depressions were found. It is said to have been
                the slave cemetery for the Pannill slaves.

PARRISH FAMILY CEMETERY

DIRECTIONS: Route 15 North to Route 634 East for 0.3 miles.
                Right on first blacktop drive. Cemetery is on
                Right on crest of hill, beyond first house, but
                before main residence. Formerly called "The
                Glebe". NOTE: only one unreadable stone remains
                but there are apparently many graves. Formerly
                had a brick wall capped with rounded brick.
                The cemetery was old and in about the same condi-
                tion in 1930 when property last changed hands.

PORTER FAMILY CEMETERY

DIRECTIONS: Route 20 West to Route 609 West for 2.5 miles
                to Route 644 South for 1.0 miles. Long drive
                left leads to house for permission and directions.
                This cemetery is behind the original (1751 - 1753)
                house. It is said past owners at one time sold
                the tombstones for a mill. No markers or records
                remain.

OLD PORTER CEMETERY IN WOODS

DIRECTIONS: As above, except this cemetery is no inaccessible
                and lies in woods behind house. Was not visited
                and there is no record of names or numbers here.

QUANN FAMILY CEMETERY

DIRECTIONS: Route 20 West to Route 692 North to second house
on right beyond Route 602. Cemetery is in front
yard.

QUANN, David   no dates   d. in his 70's [according to owner] father, husb of
Mary [stone over in 1978]
    Infant   [small depressed grave without formal marker, but with native stone]
    Mary no dates   age 76   mother, wife of David

QUANN FAMILY CEMETERY

DIRECTIONS: Route 20 West to Route 692 North for 1.4 miles
to Route 602 [unimproved road] 1.0 miles to
cemetery on right.

CHAMBERS, Harriet d. 21 Dec 1960
    Harvey C. 26 Mar 1873 - 27 Feb 1946 brother
    Kathryn ... see JAMES

JAMES, Kathryn Chambers   12 Mar 1881 - 27 Feb 1938 sister

QUANN, Anna C. 7 Sept 1882 - 29 Dec 1960   wife of G.Melvin
    G.Melvin 8 Apr 1884 - 17 Nov 1964   husb of Anna C.
    Hugh W. 1912 - 1976
    Infant b & d 7 Dec 1917   son of G. Melvin and Anna C.
    John William 4 Mar 1872 - 19 Sept 1957
    Rebecca F. 13 Jan 1854 - 7 Feb 1930
    Sarah Catherine 26 Mar 1876 - 7 Aug 1935
    Tacy A. 1917 -
    William H. 13 Apr 1850 - 15 July 1923

QUANN FAMILY CEMETERY
[ELMER KUBE PROPERTY]

DIRECTIONS: Beginning at the cemetery above, continue on
Route602 to next square white house on left.
Cemetery is on property line to West. Mr Kube
says there are no markers, but appear to have
six to eight graves.

RHOADES FAMILY CEMETERY

DIRECTIONS: Route 20 West to Route 692 North to VERLING and
             TINDER mailboxes on right [2.2 miles]. Turn right
             on farm road over cattle guard. At barns turn
             left over two more cattle guards and follow to the
             end of road to TINDER home which is the old RHOADES
             homeplace. Information given by the two Mrs.
             Tinders. Graves are not marked and are in woods
             near house. NOTE: The ladies consulted written
             records to assure accuracy.

CAWTHORNE, Eliz ... see RHOADES

HANSON, Clarinda ... see RHOADES

KUBE, Gertrude ... see RHOADES

REYNOLDS, Alville 11 Apr 1862 - 16 Apr 1881 son of Lucy Frances Reynolds
    Lucy Frances Rhoades ... see SMITH

RHOADES, Clarinda Hanson 27 Feb 1832 - 24 July 1853 single
    Elizabeth Cawthorne 29 June 1809 - Apr 1838 wife of William R.
    Gertrude Kube 25 Feb 1838 - 19 May 1930 [born in Germany] married
                        29 May 1866 to Richard "Ben" Rhoades
    Lucy Frances ... see SMITH
    Lucy Wright wife of Richard, no dates except marriage on 9 Feb 1793
    Rebecca Hanson no dates single
    Richard no dates except married 9 Feb 1793 to Lucy Wright. Will 1841
    Richard Benjamin "Ben" 12 Aug 1834 - 25 Jan 1916 married 29 May 1866 to
                        Gertrude Kube
    William Richard 4 Apr 1794 - 4 Oct 1870 husb of Elizabeth Cawthorne, son of
                        Richard and Lucy W.

SMITH, Lucy Frances Rhoades Reynolds 16 Jan 1837 - Mar 1911 "Aunt Fanny"
                        second husb was Marcellus Smith who is buried at
                        Zoar Baptist Church Cemetery

WRIGHT, Lucy ... see RHOADES

RHOADES CEMETERY ON ROUTE 692

DIRECTIONS: Route 20 West to Route 692 North for 3.2 miles.
             On left is a cemetery "at the turn of the road"
             which is an old Rhoades cemetery. Informant: Mrs.
             Tinder.

RHOADES, John b. 1776 death date not known no stone
    Susan Rhoades [a cousin, second wife of John] no dates, no marker

RHOADES SLAVE CEMETERY

DIRECTIONS: Route 20 West to Route 692 North to TINDER and
VERLING mail boxes. Turn right and at barns turn
left crossing three cattle guards. Cemetery
directions and permission at TINDER house. Informant: Mrs Tinder. NOTE: no stones.

RICHARDSON FAMILY CEMETERY

DIRECTIONS: From Unionville Route 669 South to Route 612 West
to Shady Grove Baptist Church. North on Route 677
for 0.05 miles beyond church. Cemetery is to left
behind a mobile home.

RICHARDSON, Edward H. sr 8 Oct 1920 - 19 Mar 1945 Va T/5 QMC WW II
Tucker 14 Nov 1889 - 25 May 1968 Va Pvt Co I 525 Eng SVC Bn WW I

ROACH FAMILY CEMETERY

DIRECTIONS: Route 33 West to Route 644 North for 0.02 miles.
Park at Union Grove Church.   Cemetery is in grove
of trees in field across from church. Permission
from Herndon's ROLLING WOOD FARM which is last
drive on North of Route 33 before Route 644.
No stones, but this farm was originally a ROACH
homeplace.

ROACH - PEREGORY CEMETERY

DIRECTIONS: Route 20 West to Route 609 West to Route 610
North. This cemetery is badly overgrown and
lies to the East of the house on corner of Route
609 and Route 610. Ask permission at house.
NOTE: No PEREGORY stones were found, but the
owner said it was indeed a PEREGORY cemetery.

ROACH, Annie Florence 26 Oct 1863 - 20 Feb 1905 wife of John L.
John Lewis 7 Sept 1862 - 6 Apr 1931 husb of Annie F.

ROBERTS - RHOADES FAMILY CEMETERY

DIRECTIONS: Directly across road from Herman May home in
GREENE COUNTY on Route 657 is a farm road to the
Northeast. This brings you back into Orange
COUNTY. Cemetery is across stream feeding farm
pond and then 100 yards uphill. Badly overgrown.
May be more stones. Informant: Herman May who
is relative to all in this cemetery.

RHOADES, Gillie M. 28 June 1862 - 11 June 1893 wife of Samuel Rhoades,
                    maternal grandmother of Herman May
    Samuel 17 Nov 1854 - 23 Sept 1919 husb of Gillie M. grandfather of informant

ROBERTS, Inf child of Robert Roberts no stone
    Robert   no stone father of infant son

THOMPSON, Ella no stone wife of Robert Thompson, mother of infant son
    Infant son of Robert and Ella Thompson no stone
    Robert   no stone husb of Ella, father of inf son

WATSON, Elmer   no stone   cousin to informant

ROLLINS FAMILY CEMETERY

DIRECTIONS: Route 20 West to Route 631 Southwest to Route 612
South for 0.2 miles to cemetery on left. Owner
for permission lives in second house on next road
to left.

CRANE, Ethel ... see ROLLINS

DORFMEYER, Children [two] buried c. 1958]

FINCH, Arthur Lee 13 Apr 1925 - 1 July 1951 Va S/1 USNR WW II
    Glen Allen 2 Dec 1958 - 20 Dec 1958

INMAN, Mary ... see LYNCH

LYNCH, Mary Inman 4 Mar 1886 - 9 Jan 1959 wife of William A.
    William Anderson 3 May 1877 - 25 May 1955 husb of Mary I.

ROLLINS, Ethel Crane 8 Apr 1885 - 4 Jan 1956 wife of James W. sr
    James A. 30 Apr 1852 - 14 Apr 1932
    James A. 12 Dec 1933 - 19 Aug 1959
    James William sr 7 Mar 1885 - 9 Jan 1967 husb of Ethel C.
    Mary Alice 23 Oct 1938 - 6 Jan 1939

SANFORD FAMILY CEMETERY

DIRECTIONS: Route 522 North from Route 20 to Route 701 West
to Route 617 North to first farm road on left.
0.3 miles is a gate on left. Follow through field
to old barn. Park. Walk past barns to old house
foundation. Cemetery is on right about 50 yards
from house foundation. It is fenced, in wooded
area.

SANFORD, Lawrence 2 June 1817 – 11 Nov 1898 husb of Lucy H.
Lucy H. 21 Sept 1824 – 27 Nov 1915 wife of Lawrence
Lulie 12 Apr 1861 – 25 Sept 1880

WALKER, James age 8 years [dates difficult to read ? 1872 – 1880?] son of
Mary S. and P.T. Walker
Marion age 3 weeks d. 1870 dau P.T. and M.S. Walker
Mary S. 25 Mar 1847 – 3 Aug 1873 wife of P.T. Walker

SAUNDERS CEMETERY

DIRECTIONS: Note: this cemetery was on the "Billy Young"
property , but has been moved.

BROCKMAN, Lucy Q. no dates

SAUNDERS, Francis Jones 19 Feb 1813 – 10 Mar 1894   1st Lt Inf & 2nd Div CSA

SCHULER PLACE FAMILY CEMETERY

DIRECTIONS: Route 20 West from Orange to Route 231 South to
Route 705 West for 0.54 miles to school bus turn
around. Park. Walk through field to hickory
tree and walled cemetery. Permission at Somerset
Plantation # 1   Mr. Henry Powell, informant.

CRITTENDEN, William d. 27 Mar 1817 age 88 yrs footstone "W.C."

WEBB, A. d. 1897
Fannie Vivion d. 29 Aug 1816 age 23 dau of A. Webb
Lia d . 1829 [rest of stone too weathered to read]

other unmarked graves and several graves marked with native stone.

SHIFFLETT FAMILY CEMETERY

DIRECTIONS: Route 33 West to next road to left beyond Route
              664. This appears to be an extension of Route
              652, but it is a farm road. Go about 0.05 miles
              and bear left at the botton of a hill through
              a chained gate. Close the gate! Cement steps on
              right at top of hill lead to the cemetery.

BREEDEN, Hiram Assie 25 May 1884 - 12 Apr 1957
    Louisa Frances 1862 - 1950 88 years

LAMB, Ruby ... see SHIFFLETT

SHIFFLETT, George D. 27 Mar 1948 - 17 Apr 1974
    George N. 5 Sept 1913 - 7 Apr 1972
    Lillie Florence 1882 - 1965 mother
    Nora C. 12 Apr 1919 - 30 Dec 1959
    Ruby Lamb 1922 -   wife of Rufus J.
    Rufus Jackson 1916 - 1971 husb of Ruby L.

SIMMONS FAMILY CEMETERY

DIRECTIONS: Not given. From obituary

SIMMONS, Barbara Jackson 10 May 1875 - 29 June 1978 wid of Cyrus Simmons
                          dau of Preston and Tabby Smith Jackson
    Cyrus no dates

SIMMS - TERRILL FAMILY CEMETERY

DIRECTIONS: Route 522 South to Route 629 West to Route 649
              South to 3rd drive on right. This is 1.2 miles.
              Informant and Owner: Oliver Simms.

EUSTACE, Elizabeth ... see TERRILL

SIMMS, Edmund R. 30 Oct 1861 - 1 Mar 1934 husb of Mattie J.
    Edmund Richard jr 26 Dec 1894 - 1 Apr 1945
    Elizabeth [Miss.] 7 July 1898 - 25 Sept 1970
    Mattie J. 11 May 1871 - 28 Aug 1944 wife of Edmund R.

TERRILL, Elizabeth Eustace 9 Apr 1801 - 21 Aug 1890 wife of John Terrill
    John 12 May 1791 - 9 Sept 1873 husb of Elizabeth Eustace

SISSON FAMILY CEMETERY

DIRECTIONS: Route 3 West to Route 601. At fork bear right on
Route 603 for 3.4 miles. Watch for mailbox on
left labeled "Ducker". House is across the street.
Mr Ducker will give permission and directions.
NOTE: There are many other graves without markers.

HUME, Lizzie ... see SISSON

SISSON, Joseph Quinton 3 Sept 1852 - 20 May 1904 footstone "JQS"
Laura Caroline 16 Jan 1916 - 28 Dec 1928
Lizzie Hume 29 Jan 1870 - 31 May 1962
Mildred Hannah 21 Nov 1857 - 21 May 1933

SLAUGHTER - WILLIS - BULL CEMETERY

DIRECTIONS: In Orange from Route 20 North on Selma to High
School. As you face the school, last road to
left leads to bus turn-around and gas pump. The
cemetery is on the hill above the gas pump. It is
thought to have been a Greenfield Cemetery. Many
stones have been overturned. It is poor condition.

BULL, Harriette Peyton 5 Jan 1853 - 16 Nov 1853 age 10 months 11 days dau of
Marcus and Sarah T.D. Bull
Nellie ... see WILLIS

GRYMES, J. Edgar "born" no date   "died" no date. [Large stone tipped over
within iron fenced area in larger cemetery]

SLAUGHTER, Lester 19 May 1874 - 5 Aug 1874 on same side of obelisk as Mercer
Mary L. 3 June 1875 - 17 June 1879 on same side of obelisk as Sidney N.
Mary S. 3 July 1845 - 10 Dec 1886 alone on one side of obelisk
Mercer 29 Oct 1871 - 9 Feb 1872 on obelisk with Lester
Sidney N. 30 Mar 1877 - 13 Aug 1877 on obelisk with Mary L.

WILLIS, Nellie 11 May 1848 - 27 Apr 1882 born in Orange married 4 Nov 1881
to H. Lee Willis. [Other side of obelisk could not be
read as it was facing the ground. It did have lettering.]

SMITH FAMILY CEMETERY

DIRECTIONS: Route 522 South to Route 629 East to Route 651 North
to second farm road on left beyond Route 624.
Cemetery is across from this road. Informant:
Clarence Smith. NOTE: There are as many as 20
graves.

SMITH, Gladys V. 1909 - 1975 mother of Clarence Smith

SMITH, Louisa d. ca. 1930 grandmother of Clarence Smith
   Luticia d. ca. 1920 great-grandmother of informant

SNIPER GRAVE

DIRECTIONS: Route 522 South to Route 629 East to Route 651
             East to Route 692 North. 0.5 miles North on the
             left is an old gray house and a large oak tree.
             The grave was exposed during a storm and was
             moved back 25 feet under the tree from which the
             Sniper is said to have fallen. Informant: Clyde
             Johnson. Also a young woman who lives on the
             corner of Route 692 and Route 651. NOTE: This
             is a different SNIPER GRAVE from the one in
             Spotsylvania County which was recorded in a
             carving on the tree.

SOLDIER'S REST

DIRECTIONS: Route 522 North to Route 663 North to Route 611
             East to Route 620 North [first entrance, it is a
             loop road] for 1.2 miles. The red brick two
             storied house is un occupied. Cemetery is over-
             grown and has recently had several stones removed
             to another cemetery. There are many sunken un-
             marked graves as well as 8 - 10 native stones.
             The circle in front of the house is said to have
             contained the remains of many Revolutionary
             soldiers. Hence, the name SOLDIER'S REST.

BRUCE, Charles [Capt.] d. 1792

MORTON, Dr. George and family no dates

WILLIAMS, James [Capt.] 1758 - 1822

SPOTSWOOD FAMILY CEMETERY

DIRECTIONS: Route 3 West to Lake - of - the - Woods entrance
             on left. Get permission and directions from
             security. Cemetery is on Spotswood drive near
             entrance. There are six or more unmarked graves.

GORDON, Lucy ... see SPOTSWOOD

SPOTSWOOD, Alexander Dandridge 19 Nov 1836 - 8 Dec 1924
   Alexander Gordon 10 Sept 1873 - 16 Feb 1917 son of Lucy G. and Alexander D.
   Lucy Gordon 18 June 1836 - 8 Feb 1922

SULLIVAN FAMILY CEMETERY

DIRECTIONS: Mine Run South on Route 608 for 1.7 miles. Wheeler
              Farm is on right. Cemetery is fenced in front yard
              of home.

SULLIVAN, Cameller 12 Apr 1875 – 8 July 1928 Mother
    Infants [two] buried beside mother

TATUM CEMETERY ON CARTER PLACE

DIRECTIONS: Route 522 South to Route 629 East to Route 651
              North. Cemetery is fenced, beside house on
              Southwest corner of Route 651 and Route 624.

TATUM, Ada B. 23 Sept 1877 – 9 Jan 1947 wife of Robert H.
    Robert H. 15 May 1866 – 25 July 1933 husb of Ada B.

TAYLOR CEMETERY AT BLOOMSBURY
[JOHNSON - QUARLES]

DIRECTIONS: See JERDONE CEMETERY for directions.

JOHNSON, David 7 Apr 1777 – ____st June 1823
    Nancy d. 9 May 1854 age 48 yrs wife of Dr. Peter T. Johnson

QUARLES, Lucy 28 Feb 1773 – 23 Aug 1841 wife of William
    William 9 Oct 1765 – 13 Aug 1834 husb of Lucy

TAYLOR CEMETERY AND MONUMENT AT MEADOW FARM

DIRECTIONS: Route 20 to Route 612 South for 1.5 miles to
              fifth drive on left. MEADOW FARM on gate pillars.
              Bear right to house for permission and directions.

ASHBY, Roberta ... see TAYLOR

EARNEST, Betsy Hord Taylor 23 Sept 1818 –   dau of Edmund P. and
                     Mildred E. Taylor m. 30 Dec 1851 to Joseph Earnest

EARNEST, Edmund Taylor 28 June 1856 – 29 July 1879 son of Betsy H. and
                Joseph Earnest
    Josephine 12 May 1853 – 30 Dec 1877 dau of Betsy Hord and Joseph Earnest

HART, Jane F. 9 Jan 1800 – 20 July 1867 youngest dau of R. & F. Taylor, married
                15 Aug 1826 to John Hart

LEE, Elizabeth 1709 – 1753" wife of Zachary Taylor, dau of Hancock Lee of
                Ditchley, granddaughter of Richard Lee, grandmother
                of President Zachary Taylor, Great Aunt of President
                James Madison, great grandmother of Sarah Knox
                Taylor, wife of President Jefferson Davis of the Con-
                federacy"

PENDLETON, Frances ... see TAYLOR

PUGH, Caroline McNeill 29 July 1859 – 10 Jan 1863 dau of John W. and Ada C.
                Jennings Pugh

REVELEY, Edmund Pendleton 13 Feb 1845 – 18 July 1845 son of Robinette Taylor
                and Thomas Reveley
    Graham Aug 1860 – June 1861 son of Robinette Taylor and Thomas Reveley
    Mildred Turner 21 Aug 1848 – 18 Nov 1848 dau of Robinette Taylor and Thomas
                Reveley

RICHARDSON, Martha E. ... see TAYLOR

SHEPHERD, Lucinda A. Taylor ... see TAYLOR

TALIAFERRO, Mildred 27 Aug 1787 – 30 Mar 1854 wife of Hay Taliaferro married
                7 Feb 1805

TAYLOR, Alexander F. 4 Mar 1807 – 4 Aug 1871
    Edmund P. [Dr.] 17 Sept 1791 – 6 Oct 1840 "intermarried with Mildred E.
                Turner"
    Erasmus 29 July 1830 – 20 May 1907 son of Edmund Pendleton and Mildred E.
                Taylor, married 17 Dec 1851 to Roberta S. Ashby
    Frances Pendleton 18 Sept 1767 – 20 Oct 1831 consort of Robert Taylor,
                married 7 July 1784
    Howard 22 May 1810 – 6 Dec 1833
    Isabelle Macnish 5 Mar 1859 – 7 Jan 1861 dau of Erasmus and Roberta A.
                Taylor
    James Longstreet 17 Mar 1864 – 16 Jan 1867 son of Erasmus and Roberta A.
                Taylor
    Jaquelin P. 20 Jan 1797 – 21 Jan 1872 married Martha E. Richardson
                15 Apr 1823
    Jaquelin P. 25 Nov 1857 – 22 Feb 1858 son of Erasmus and Roberta A. Taylor
    Lucinda A. 27 Apr 1794 – 1 June 1873 second dau of Robert and Frances
                Taylor, married to James Shepherd October 1824
    Lucy Jane 21 Jan 1828 – 16 Feb 1869 youngest dau of E.P. and M.E. Taylor
    Martha E. 15 Jan 1801 – 28 Jan 1881 maried Jaquelin P. Taylor 15 Apr 1823
    Mary C. married Robert Taylor 30 July 1806
    Mary Edmonia 29 Oct 1824 – 30 Sept 1892 dau of Edmund P. and Mildred E.
                Taylor
    Mildred Edmonia 29 Sept 1799 – 20 July 1882 dau of Reuben and Elizabeth
                Pendleton Turner, married Edmund Pendleton Taylor
                23 Dec 1817
    Robert 29 Apr 1763 – 3 July 1845 intermarried with Frances Pendleton on
                7 July 1784
    Robert 30 May 1785 – 24 Sept 1846 married Mary C. Taylor 30 July 1806
    Roberta Ashby 3 Feb 1830 – 10 July 1893 dau of John and Mary Ashby, wife of
                Erasmus Taylor

TAYLOR, Zachary   1707 - 1768 "son of James Taylor II, of Bloomsbury, Knight
                of the Golden Horseshoe. Grand parent of President
                Zachary Taylor, Great Uncle of President James
                Madison, Great Grand parent of Sara Knox Taylor,
                wife of President Jefferson Davis of the Confederacy,
                husband of Elizabeth Lee."

TURNER, Mildred Edmonia ... see TAYLOR

CEMETERY ON TENSMORE PROPERTY

DIRECTIONS: Route 20 West to Route 611 to Route 620 (loop road)
              where cemetery is on inner loop at house once
              called "Island View". Three stones were recently
              moved to Mt Holy Cemetery. Informant: Clyde
              Johnson

TERRELL FAMILY CEMETERY

DIRECTIONS: Route 20 West to Route 231 South to Route 654 then
              Northwest on Route 732 to first road on right.
              Farm road extends for 0.9 miles to cemetery on
              left. Recorded by owner, Mrs. June Funkhouser.

TERRELL, Buckner 22 Feb 1788 - 2 July 1854 father
     Glanville 20 Oct 1859 - 4 Oct 1936 son of Oliver and Mary J. Terrell
     Howard Macaulay 3 Jan 1866 - 13 Jan 1900 son of Oliver and Mary J. Terrell
     Jane S. d. 22 Mar 1832 33 years of age, mother, wife of Buckner Terrell
     Junius S. 12 Mar 1832 - 17 Mar 1833
     Lucy Ann 1829 - 1837 8 years 6 days
     Mary J. 9 Oct 1833 - 16 July 1896 wife of Oliver H. P. Terrell
     O.H.P. jr 22 May 1868 - 12 Nov 1895 son of Oliver and Mary J. Terrell
     Oliver H.P. 14 Nov 1830 - 9 Mar 1922
     Percy T. 25 Sept 1863 - 6 May 1884 son of Oliver and Mary J. Terrell
     Sarah Jerdone 20 Feb 1858 - 27 Oct 1942 dau of O.H.P. and M.J. Terrell

TETLEY MANOR WHITE FLOWER GARDEN CEMETERY

DIRECTIONS: Route 20 West to Route 231 North to Route 641 East
              to Tetley Manor on left. Walled garden with white
              flowers and cherubs. Ask permission.

ERIKSEN, Louise Close d. 13 June 1958 [later moved to Washington, D.C.] Poem
              written by Mrs. Eriksen. "Flowers flowers lovely
              flowers, Gems on Earth so bright and gay, There is
              much that they can teach us, There is much that they
              can say, List and you shall hear their voices, Speaking
              to us from the sod, List and they shall lead you gently
              Upward from this Earth to God." by L.C.E.

THOMPSON CEMETERY

DIRECTIONS: On the William S. Thompson place, behind the
LUMSDEN CEMETERY. Can only be reached by four
wheel drive vehicle. Informant: Clyde Johnson
Not visited.

THURSTON FAMILY CEMETERY

DIRECTIONS: On the corner of Route 741 and Route 602 across
from Rhoadesville Postoffice. Informant Mr.
Thurston, No stones.

CARTER, Georgia ... see THURSTON

THURSTON, Georgia Carter d. ca. 1970 wife of Reuben
Reuben d. ca. 1966 husb of Georgia Carter

TIMBERLAKE CEMETERY AT HICKS

DIRECTIONS: Located near Mine Run off Route 608 across from
Walt Sullivan's Store. Cemetery is in deep woods
and has not been used for many years. Informant:
Keith Walters.

TIMBERLAKE, Chapman no dates Coleman's battery CSA

TINSLEY FAMILY CEMETERY

DIRECTIONS: From Burr Hill Store South on Route 692 for 0.5
miles to Cemetery on right side of road. In
addition to recorded stones, there are 11 native
stone markers and 5+ unmarked graves.

SPICER, William Earl 16 Nov 1905 – 17 Apr 1928

TINSLEY, A.H.S. no dates
    G.H.T. no dates
    Henry E. no dates Co I 6th Va Cav CSA
    H.E.T. no dates
    T.A. no dates

TURNER - ALMOND CEMETERY

DIRECTIONS: Route 20 West to Route 611 South to Route 604
South to Route 608 South. Cemetery is behind the
Dempsey home which is next house East of Walt
Sullivan's Store on same side of road.

ALMOND, Liston V. no dates Co I 6 Va Cav CSA

SULLIVAN, Myrtle 29 Mar 1899 - 19 Mar 1978

TURNER, Charles E. 19 June 1877 - 30 Nov 1946 Uncle
H.W. no dates Co C 6 Va Cav CSA

WALLACE FAMILY CEMETERY

DIRECTIONS: Same as above, but 0.05 miles from Spotsylvania
County Line on left.

CLARKE, Beulah Leona d. 7 Dec 1977 age 46 years

SULLIVAN, EMMA ... see WALLACE

WALLACE, Emma Sullivan d. 23 May 1975 age 77 years wife of John D.
   Irvin F. 29 June 1937 - 21 Dec 1937 son of J.D. and E. M. Wallace
   John D. 27 June 1894 - 22 Mar 1978 b. in Spotsylvania, d. in Fredericksburg
      son of Festus and Margaret Owens Wallace, husb of
      Emma Sullivan Wallace
   John R. 12 June 1920 - 23 Nov 1943 Va Pvt 1072 D. Guard Squ Air Corps
      WW II

WASHINGTON FAMILY CEMETERY

DIRECTIONS: Route 20 West to Route 621 to Route 602 West for
0.1 miles to cemetery on right. NOTE: This is
an old family cemetery, fenced, in good condition,
but with many many more graves than headstones or
other markers.

HILL, Alice 1919 - 1960

RANDOLPH, Mary 1890 - 1972
   Wallace 1912 - 1952

ROBERTS, Julia Washington 1907 - 7 Aug 1978 dau of Wesley and Mattie Payne
      Washington, wife of Edgar Roberts of Philadelphia

SMITH, Annie 1934 – 1978 age 43 years

WASHINGTON, John d. 23 June 1959 age 66 years
    Julia ... see ROBERTS
    Margaret 1917 – 1976 Mother
    Roger Lee 5 July 1934 – 7 Sept 1972 38 years Va Cpl USA

WAUGH FAMILY CEMETERY ON BUSH MOUNTAIN FARM

DIRECTIONS: Route 20 West to Route 522 North to Route 701
West to Route 617/627 West to Route 626 North to
first farm road on left. At end of road cemetery
is on right near barns. Walled, well cared for.

GARDNER, Emily J. Waugh ... see WAUGH
    George Morgan 7 Dec 1820 – 1 Feb 1918
    J. [James] M. 24 Sept 1844 – 18 Mar 1912 husb of Emily J.
    Myrtle 7 Dec 1888 – 21 Aug 1910 "Our Darling" dau of James M. and Emily
        Gardner

PALMER, Nora ... see WAUGH

PANNILL, Joseph B. [Capt] no dates Co F Va Res CSA husb of Fannie B.
    Williams

PRIEST, Albert Tellous 23 Feb 1847 – 7 Oct 1925 husb of Mary E.
    Eleanor 18 Apr 1885 – 30 Sept 1889 "Little Jeannie"
    Mary E. 30 Oct 1847 – 25 Sept 1913 wife of Albert T.

WAUGH, Charles S. 22 Oct 1823 – 30 Dec 1908 85 yr 2 mo 7 ds husb of Mary
    Cora L. 12 Apr 1866 – 15 Mar 1892 25 yr 11 mo 3 ds wife of G.E.Waugh
    Emily J. 7 Mar 1853 – 6 Dec 1917 wife of James M. Gardner
    Garrett E. 16 Jan 1896 – 11 Apr 1918 son of G.E. and Nora P. Waugh
    George Morgan 18 May 1861 – 16 Oct 1899 son of Chas S. and Mary F. Waugh
    Goree E. 21 Dec 1857 – 12 Apr 1935 husb of 1] Cora L. and 2] Nora P.
    Mary 17 Sept 1823 – 17 Nov 1882 wife of C.S. Waugh
    Nora Lee 6 Mar 1907 – 15 Mar 1907
    Nora Palmer 4 Mar 1872 – 9 Nov 1920 second wife of G.E. Waugh
    Sarah b. Nov 1891 age 6 years, "A Methodist"

WAUGH - PANNILL CEMETERY

DIRECTIONS: Route 522 North to farm road on right just before
Route 701. [New brick house drive just beyond the
correct one.] Property owned by Andrew and Virginia
Coleman. Cemetery has high concrete wall and no
gate.

PANNILL, Two wives, both moved to Graham recently

RHOADES, Baby [probably child of Mrs. L.A. Rhoades
    L.A. [Mrs.] dates unknown

TINDER, Bertha ... see WAUGH

WAUGH, Bertha Tinder no known dates wife of Charlie
    Charlie dates unknown husb of Bertha Tinder
    wife of _____ also moved to Graham recently

WEBB - ROGERS FAMILY CEMETERY

DIRECTIONS: 1.5 miles South of Airport on Route 20. Huey
                Richards in nearest house does not own property,
                but gave permission to cross his grounds. This
                cemetery is about 100 yards West of the NEWMAN
                FAMILY CEMETERY, across two fences.

ROGERS, _____[rest of stone buried]
    Ernest B. 31 Dec _____ - _ July ___
    Mary A. 2 Mar 1832 - 25 July 1894

WEBB, F. L. d. 3 June 18 [2?] 9 age 35 years [11?] mo
    John d. 28 Oct 1866 age 60 years

?? [partial stone] 2 Apr 1827 - 30 Dec 187 [?]

WHITLOCK - ADKINS FAMILY CEMETERY

DIRECTIONS: Route 20 West to Route 631 West to Route 612
                South to Route 622. Left in farm road opposite
                Route 622. House at end of drive. Cemetery is
                some distance back in woods on trail. Informant:
                Mrs. Jesse Sacra. Cemetery was not visited. There
                are no stones. Mrs Sacra was Jane Seal.

ADKINS, Joe "last one buried, a long time ago" according to Mrs. Sacra
    Martha ... see WHITLOCK

PENDLETON, Betty ... see WHITLOCK

SEAL, Frances no dates, sister of Mrs Jane Seal Sacra, she married a Toonan
    Rosala died young, sister of Mrs Sacra

TOONAN, Frances Seal ... see SEAL

WHITLOCK, Betty no dates, Aunt of Mrs Sacra. She married a Pendleton
    Grandfather of Mrs Sacra no dates
    Grandmother of Mrs Sacra no dates
    Martha Aunt who married an Adkins

WILKINS - PEYTON FAMILY CEMETERY

DIRECTIONS: Route 15 North to Route 632 East to Route 700 North
beyond paved portion of road. When in sight of
RR at sharp right turn there are two gates, one
straight ahead, one to your left. Park in front
of left gate. Through gate, approximately 0.5
miles to river on path that once was a road. Then
left along ridge beside river for approximately
0.3 miles to cemetery on left. All stones down.
Difficult to spot. Find foundation for house
and go 50 yards to left for easiest location.
Permission from Mr. Sanford, farm manager. NOTE:
A letter from Annie Laws Ashton Carpenter [Mrs.
Ralph Lester Carpenter] born 22 Nov 1901 at this
farm gave much additional information as well as
genealogical information of Peyton-Wilkins
families for five generations. That material
follows the cemetery record. NOTE ALSO: Only
WILKINS stones remain.

LEWIS, Nellie ... see WILKINS

PEYTON, Anna Dade 3 Aug 1821 - 24 May 1917
Cora Lee no dates inf dau of Sarah E.R. & Thomas J. Peyton
George Washington 26 Oct 1828 - 8 Feb 1887
Henry Llewellyn 12 Jan 1836 - 2 Mar 1880 husb of 1] Mary Eliza Pauli and
2] Lenora Keefe, actress
Infants, two, of Thomas Jefferson Peyton and Sarah Elizabeth Reynolds Peyton
John 5 May 1793 - 2 May 1862 b. Stafford County married 9 Nov 1815 by
Rev. Kobler, Madison County, Va., to Lydia Price
Snyder
Lucy F. ... see WILKINS
Lydia Price Snyder 13 Mar 1796 - 4 Apr 1896 wife of John, dau of Michael
and Martha Stigler Snyder of Madison County, Va.
Mary Jane 5 July 1825 - 6 Aug 1908

SMITH, Mr. no dates

SNYDER, Lydia Price ... see PEYTON

WILKINS, John Peyton 26 Aug 1858 - 4 Aug 1890 born Warrenton, Va.
John Quincy Adams 30 Sept 1830 - 19 Mar 1898 husb of Lucy Frances Peyton
Kate May 10 May 1870 - 14 July 1894 footstone "KMW"
Lucy F. Peyton 15 Nov 1829 - 24 Apr 1898 footstone "LFW" wife of John Q.A.
Nellie Lewis 26 May 1861 - 23 May 1863 footstone "NLW"

ASHTON - PEYTON - SNYDER - WILKINS GENEALOGY
[ACCORDING TO ANNIE LAWS ASHTON CARPENTER]

16 August 1978

PEYTON, John born 5 May 1793 Stafford County, Virginia died 2 May 1862 in
Orange County, Virginia. Married 9 November 1815
by Rev. Kobler, Madison Courthouse, Virginia with
records there.

SNYDER, Lydia Price born 13 March 1796 Madison County, Virginia. Died
4 April 1896 Orange County, daughter of Michael and
Martha Stigler Snyder. Married John Peyton,above,
and lived at Rapidan where he worked for Spotswood
and Taliaferro's mill later known as Holliday's Mill.
In 1817 they moved 3 miles from Orange on the
Rapidan and bought 7 acres where he and General Dade
ran a [Flour - Grist] mill and a Lime Kiln on the Madison
side of the river. He patented a blower to blow away
husk from corn, etc. The patent is signed by John
Quincy Adams, Pres. 1825. Document is owned by
Mrs. Carpenter.
Lydia and John had 12 children, and she lived to be
100 years and 21 days. My mother, Lutta Wilkins Ashton,
lived with her grandmother Lydia and bought the place
and stayed there until two maiden Aunts passed away.
The mill washed away during a flood. I do not know
the date. It is known as Peyton's Ford, but the Family
always called it Rock Mills or Rocky Mills.

My grandmother, Lucy Frances Peyton, my mother, Lutta Erwin Wilkins Ashton
and me were born there.

CHILDREN OF JOHN AND LYDIA PEYTON

1. William Snyder Peyton 4 Dec 1816 - 30 Jan 1899 married Willie Ann Newman
8 children
2. John Stigler Peyton 1 Nov 1819 - 1901 [died Staunton River] married Harriet
Dowell and 2] Sara Martha Newman 6 children
3. Anna Dade Peyton 3 Aug 1821 - 24 May 1917 unmaried, raised a nephew,
buried at Peyton's Ford
4. James Franklin Peyton 16 Jan 1823 moved to Hinton, West Virginia no record
5. Mary Jane Peyton 5 July 1825 - 6 Aug 1908 unmarried buried at Peyton's Ford
6. George Washington Peyton 26 Oct 1828 - 8 Feb 1887 twin to Georgiana, unmarried, buried at Peyton's Ford, watchman at Fat Nancy
Trestle
7. Georgiana Peyton 26 Oct 1828 [death date not known] married John Jones
Robinson
8. Lucy Frances Peyton 15 Nov 1829 - 28 Apr 1898 married John Quincy Adams
Wilkins [birthdate not known] d. Mar 1898. He was
from Eastern Shore of Maryland.
CHILDREN OF Lucy Frances Peyton and John Quincy Adams Wilkins

a. Nellie Lewis 26 May 1861 - 23 May 1863 buried at Peyton's Ford
b. John Peyton 26 Aug 1858 - 4 Aug 1890 buried at Peyton's Ford
c. Nannie Gordon Wilkins 11 July 1862 - 5 Apr 1912 married Alvin
Morton Wattles, buried Alexandria, Va., one dau,
Ouida Breston, Cin., O. retired nurse, living
d. My Mother, Lutta Erwin Wilkins 28 May 1865 - 22 Nov 1948 married
Henry C. Ashton of Orange. She buried in Alex-
andria, Va., he in Hollywood, Cal. 2 children:
Conway Glassell Ashton 29 Dec 1899 - 16 June
1957 married Henrietta Louise Shirkey 2 children;
me: Annie Laws Ashton 22 Nov 1901- married
11 July 1943 Ralph Lester Carpenter from Madison,
Virginia. I was born at Peyton's Ford, all my
childhood there.
e. Magnus Taliaferro Wilkins 4 Apr 1868 - 18 Dec 19-- born in Alexandria, buried Herndon, Virginia. married Cora
Lewis 2 children: Lucy Virginia Wilkins 1 Nov 1898-
16 Apr 1961, and Magnus Waite Wilkins 25 Aug 1906
married Virginia Lang, live at Stephen's City, Va
f. Kate May Wilkins 10 May 1870 - 14 July 1894 unmarried, buried
at Peyton's Ford

g. James Edward Wilkins 23 Aug 1873 – [death date unknown] buried
      Herndon, Virginia married Mary Laws
9. Eliza Penelope [Nellie] Peyton 6 June 1831 died in childbirth. Child raised
      by Grandmother Lydia and Aunt Ann. Married to
      James Fontaine Kennedy. buried in Orange County
10. Thomas Jefferson Peyton 22 July 1833 – 28 Mar 1910 married Sarah Elizabeth
      Reynolds [Sally Betty] 10 children three died in infancy
      [they buried at Peyton's Ford]
11. Henry Llewellyn Peyton 12 Jan 1836 – 2 Mar 1880 married 1] Mary Eliza Pauli
      and 2] Leonore Keefe actress. Buried at Peyton's Ford
12. Virginia Helena Peyton 3 Sept 1838 – April 1915 born Peyton's Ford, died
      at Alexandria , Virginia. Married John Francis
      Chauncey; he had 5 sons from previous marriage. They
      had 3 children.

WILLIS CEMETERY ON KUBE DAIRY FARM

DIRECTIONS: Route 3 West to Route 601. Turn left for 1.0
miles. At fork bear left on 601 for another 1.0
miles. At sharp left turn in road continue
straight ahead on farm road [Rural Box #69] to
house and directions for cemetery.

GARNETT, Irene ... see GORDON

GORDON, Irene Garnett 14 Oct 1855 – 11 Apr 1899 Our Loving Mother
Irene Woodford 10 Mar 1893 – 22 Nov 1933
Mary ... see WILLIS
Sallie Willis 17 June 1867 – 11 July 1936

WILLIS, John Churchill 21 May 1824 – 2 Aug 1894 Pastor of Flat Run Baptist
Church from April 1853 to 2 Aug 1894 husb of Mary
Gatesby Woodford
Larkin 26 Feb 1801 – 21 Feb 1856 husb of Mary Gordon
Mary Gatesby Woodford 8 June 1822 – 3 Aug 1894 wife of John Churchill Willis
Mary Gordon 4 Mar 1807 – 2 Nov 1881 wife of Larkin
Sallie ... see GORDON
WOODFORD, Irene ... see GORDON
Mary Gatesby ... see WILLIS

WILTSHIRE FAMILY CEMETERY

DIRECTIONS: Route 522 South to Route 629 East to Route 651
North for 1.3 miles. Park. On right is old farm
road blocked by logs. Walk briskly for three
minutes on path. Cemetery is on your right.

JACOBS, Lelia ... see WILTSHIRE

WILTSHIRE, Benjamin David 1882 – 1920
Lelia Jacobs 1861 – 1889 wife of Weedon M. "Sonny"

WILTSHIRE, Weedon M. jr 1888 - 1889 son of Weedon and Lelia J.
    Weedon M. "Sonny" 1859 - 1930 husb of Lelia Jacobs

WINDHOLME FARM CEMETERY #1

DIRECTIONS: Route 15 South from Orange to Route 639 West.
Get permission from house at second road on left.
NOTE: This is the former Clifton Farm

AMOS, Rosa ... see SCOTT

DENNIS, Charles Henry 1849 - 1913
    Sallie Scott 1860 - 1901

LANDRUM, Huldah 1815 - 1881
    Mary ... see SCOTT

SCOTT, Charles 1799 - 1868
    Charles Poindexter 1876 - 1895
    Delia 1852 - 1913
    Julia 1856 - 1879
    Marion 1855 - 1855
    Mary Landrum 1818 - 1900
    Rosa Amos 1861 - 1893
    Sallie ... see DENNIS

WINDHOLME FARM CEMETERY #2

DIRECTIONS: See above.

NALLE, Sarah Ellen ... see SCOTT

SCOTT, Charles 1843 - 1861
    Fanny 1831 - 1862
    Garrett 9 Apr 1808 - 24 Feb 1885 husb of Sarah Ellen Nalle, father of Fanny,
                    George, Philip, Thomas, Charles, and Mary
    George 1833 - 1852
    Jane 28 Dec 1699 - 28 Apr 1731 wife of John Scott
    Mary 1847 - 1848
    Philip 1839 - 1871 CSA
    Sarah Ellen Nalle 1812 - 1877 wife of Garrett Scott, mother of Fanny, George,
                    Philip, Thomas, Charles, and Mary
    Thomas 1840 - 1864 CSA

WOLFORD HOUSE CEMETERY

Directions: Not given. There are ten or twelve graves mostly
marked with fieldstone. No knowledge of who is
buried here.

WOOD'S FAMILY CEMETERY

DIRECTIONS: Route 3 West for 0.5 miles West of Lake-of-the-
Woods to Cemetery in wooded area on your left.
If you come to the Flat Run Church on left or to
the Flat Run Store on right, you have already
passed the cemetery. NOTE: There are 13 native
stones and numerous unmarked graves. Informant
for some unmarked graves: Mrs Malcolm Brooks.

LAWSON, Pearl no dates, no marker [Informant: Mrs Malcolm Brooks]
    Sarah no dates beside Welford
    Welford no dates beside Sarah

WOOD, Arthur C. 21 Sept 1926 – 29 Oct 1949 Va Pfc 3530 QM Truck Co WW II
    Caroline no dates, no marker [Informant: Mrs Malcolm Brooks]
    David no dates, no marker [Informant: Mrs Malcolm Brooks]
    Fielding d. 5 Mar 1946 age 68 years 15 days
    George Wilson d. 10 Feb 1950 age 32 years 3 months 11 days
    Mary E. 1884 – 1965
    Preston D. 24 Sept 1965 age 61 years

WYATT - McGEHEE FAMILY CEMETERY

DIRECTIONS: Route 20 West to Route 650, then immediately
bear left on Route 624 South for 5.5 miles to
concrete block walled cemetery on left. Very
nicely kept. Informant: Jack Wyatt.

ASHELY, James Romaine 15 May 1900 –   [husb of Ruth McGehee]
    Resa McGehee 12 Apr 1900 – 19 Apr 1978 dau of George C. and Mildred Hughes
                McGehee, wife of James R. Ashley [obituary]
    Ruth McGehee 12 Apr 1897 – 14 Mar 1971 wife of James R.Ashley

FRANKLIN, Edwin Abbott 26 Feb 1905 – 9 Oct 1974 [husb of Grace Wyatt]
    Grace Wyatt 16 May 1918 –   [wife of Edwin A.]

HUGHES, Mildred ... see McGEHEE

McGEHEE, Aldia ... see WYATT
    Andrew J. Mc Co G 23 Va Inf CSA   no dates
    Charles R. 3 Aug 1886 – 17 Oct 1908 age 22 years, 2 months, 14 days
    Eddie J. 25 Sept 1887 – 9 Aug 1961 Va Pfc 314 Machine Gun Bn WW I [Uncle
                to informant]
    George C. 11 May 1859 – 18 Mar 1950
    Mabel C. 12 Apr 1891 – 8 June 1917
    Maggie ... see SORRELL
    Mary 1856 – 1930 [wife of William]
    Mildred A. Hughes 31 Jan 1862 – 27 July 1933 [wife of George C., parent of
                Manna McGehee Wyatt and Resa McGehee Ashley]
    Resa ... see ASHLEY
    Ruth ... see ASHLEY

McGEHEE, Thomas J. 21 June 1895 - 13 Dec 1913 [son of W.G. and Mary J.
                    McGehee]
    William 1857 - 1931

MOORE, William W. 23 May 1904 - 13 Sept 1967 [son-in-law to Joseph Allie and
                   Maggie McGehee Sorrell]

SORRELL, Charles T. 26 June 1914 - 6 May 1924 [child of Joseph Allie Sorrell
                     and Maggie McGehee Sorrell]
    Joseph Allie 25 Feb 1860 - 28 May 1950 [husb of Maggie McGehee]
    Maggie McGehee 4 Apr 1881 - 3 Feb 1965 [wife of Joseph Allie Sorrell]

WYATT, Aldia McGehee 18 Sept 1870 - 4 June 1959 [wife of Joseph O.
    Grace ... see FRANKLIN
    Homer N. 11 Feb 1895 - 28 Nov 1958 [son of Joseph Oscar and Aldia Wyatt
    Jack 5 Dec 1928-
    ?Joseph or Jacob? [Union soldier, grandfather of Joseph] no stone
    Joseph Oscar 18 Feb 1870 - 7 Feb 1957 [husb of Aldia McGehee]
    Manna M. 28 Mar 1897 -   [wife of Homer N., mother of Grace
                     Wyatt Franklin and Jack Wyatt]
    Nancy T. 10 July 1931 - 17 June 1977 [wife of Jack Wyatt]

YOWELL - COLLINS CEMETERY ON COLVIN PLACE

            DIRECTIONS: Route 20 West to Route 609 West to Route 676 North
                         for 0.7 miles to second farm road to cemetery at
                         end of road in front of house. Mr. Colvin, Infor-
                         mant.

COLLINS, Eddie L. 1 Apr 1881 - 14 Aug 1904 son of R. Frank and Alice L. Collins
    R. Frank no dates husb of Alice Lucy Yowell, father of Eddie L.

YOWELL, Alice Lucy 20 Apr 1857 - 1 June 1932 wife of R. Frank Collins, mother
                    of Eddie L. Collins

YOWELL - COLLINS SLAVE CEMETERY ON COLVIN PLACE

            DIRECTIONS: As above, but as you look toward river and Indian
                         Mound there is an area of depressions in the field
                         that was once a slave cemetery. No stones or
                         markers. No records.

INDEX

BEAZLEY
   Sallie Morton 39

BECK
   Reuben 16

BELL
   James R. 33
   M. E. 33
   Mary T. 3

BENNETT
   Mrs. 64

BERKELEY
   Henry Robinson 3
   Nannie L. 3
   William Scott 16

BICKERS
   John M. 55
   Julia M. 16

BICKLEY
   Tomasia Myrtle 43, 44

BILLINGSLEY
   Bettie S. 63
   John Dabney 63
   John P. 63

BIRCKHEAD
   Annie V. 43
   Thomas E. 43
   Virginia L. 43

BISCOE
   A.W. 30
   Lulu Jane 30
   Sallie 39
   Susan R. 30
   Susie Wright 30
   Thomas Lawson 52
   V.A. 52
   William [Capt] 30

BISPHAM
   James Skinker 16
   Mattie Adelaid 16

BLAIR
   Bessie 69
   Georgiana 3

BLAKEY
   Ann Maria 3
   Arthur G. 52
   Charles W. 52
   Eleanor M. 52
   Ella J. 52
   George W. 52
   James H. 52
   James W. 52
   Jessica C. 52
   Katus R. [Dr] 52
   Louis P. 52
   Sarah Ann 52

BLEDSOE
   Bennett 3
   Hannah 76
   Lillian Sanders 53
   Lou Willie 16
   Lucy D. 3
   Mary 53
   Mary Cattlett Sanders 53

BLEDSOE
   Mildred H. 16
   Moses Garnett 53
   Rachel 45
   Thomas Hansford 53
   William J. 39

BOND
   John 3
   Joseph W. 39
   Lucy Tatum 3
   Mary G. 3
   R. H. 3
   Thomas W. 3
   Virginia Ann 39
   Virginia W. 3

BOOSE
   Eliza 27

BOOTON
   Mary Catlett 3
   Mildred Pendleton Williams 3
   R. Sinclair 3
   William Sinclair 3

BOSTON
   Evdora B. 16
   Henry L. 16
   Jane F. Waugh 44
   John P. 44
   Sophia S. 43, 44
   Sophia Thomas 44

BOSWELL
   C. H. 3
   Mary L. 3
   Sallie M. 3
   William J. 3

BOUGHAN
   Annie E. 16
   John Claude 16
   Lutie Blanch 16
   Nathaniel James 16

BOULWARE
   Mary 41
   Mary T. 41
   Thomas 41

BOWEN
   Ella May 16
   Emmett Wilbur 16
   Fannie Etchison 16
   Infant 16
   L.D. 16
   S. F. 16

BRADBURY
   Fannie Standard 3

BRADFORD
   John E. 3
   Virginia F. 3
   William S. 3

BRADLEY
   Edwin B. 3
   Lizzie B. 3
   Lucy Willis Talliaferro 3

BRADSHAW
   Nannie 75
   W.J. 75
   Wilmer Cowan 75

BRAGG
   Ada H. 16
   Cornelia Frances 16
   Elizabeth 16
   James R. 16
   John G. 16
   Julia A. 16
   Mary E. 16
   Maurice J. 16
   Sallie F. 16
   Virgil Thomas 16
   William B. 16

BRAXTON
   Bettie 3

BREEDEN
   Ada D. 54
   Ada Kay 54
   Elizabeth 54
   Gilbert 54
   Hiram Assie 87
   Louisa Frances 87
   Marie 54
   Paul Roosevelt 54

BRENT
   Bessie Seymour 16
   Catherine 9
   Sarah 3

BRESTON
   Ouida Wilkins 98

BRIDWELL
   Oswald H. 3
   Sallie E. 3

BRIGGS
   Ferol   60

BRISCO
   Fleming 16
   Robert 16

BRITTON
   Virginia S. 39

BROCK
   W. R. 70

BROCKMAN
   Bettie T. 37
   Edward T. 37
   Lucy Q. 86
   M. Alice Cooke 37
   Nannie 44
   W. A. 37
   William A. 37

BROOKS
   Aunts 54
   Grandmother 54
   Malcolm [Mrs.] 101

BROWN
   Alverda S. 55
   Dennis F. 55
   Edgar 55
   G.J.   55
   George E. 55
   Homassel 55
   J. Albert 55
   J. B, 55
   James F. 39
   James Stephenson 3
   Jennie Elizabeth 16

BROWN
  John W. 39
  Joseph B. 55
  Lou 55
  Mary [Polly] 44
  Mary J. 67
  Oscar P. 55
  Parke Farley 55
  Sarah Ann 55
  Seth Conner 15, 16
  Thomas H. 55
  William Neil 16
  Winifred 55

BROWNING
  G. Judson 3
  Phillip Jones 45
  Sallie Busby 45
  Sarah Thomas 3

BRUCE
  Annie Elisebeth 16
  Charles [Capt.] 89
  Hamilton L. 16
  L. W. 16
  Mamie A. 16
  Mary Alice 16
  R.L. 16
  Richard 16

BRYANT
  Anne 38
  John 38

BUCKLEY
  Margaret 16

BUCKNER
  Caldwell Calhoun 3

BUDDECKE
  Christian Theodore 17
  Julia Wilson Marriner 17

BULL
  Harriette Peyton 88
  Marcus 88
  Nellie 88
  Sarah T. D. 88

BULLOCK
  Annie D. 37

BURDETTE
  Willis 3

BURGESS
  Anna W. L. Taylor 3, 4
  Honor 4
  Thomas 4
  William W. jr   4
  William Wallace 3, 4

BURNAM
  see ... BURNHAM

BURNETT
  Cornelia 4

BURNHAM
  Alice 17
  Laura 17
  Mary E. 17

BURR
  Mollie E. 30

BURRUSS - BURRUS
  Alfred [Mrs.] 60
  J. H. [Rev.] 42
  John 4
  Lancelot 37

BUSBY
  Alice Lucas 45
  Sallie 45
  William Thomas 45

BUTLER
  A.C. 17
  Alexandria 4
  Charlote Langhorne 4
  Eliza Jane 4
  M. A. 17
  M. Alice 17
  Mary A. [Mrs.] 17

CALDWELL
  Maggie 4

CAMMACK
  Flora May 35
  George W. 35, 36
  Maria T. 39
  Mary Jane Pidgeon 35
  Nellie R. 35

CAMPBELL
  America W. 56
  Elizabeth Waters 56
  Frederick W. 56
  Mary P. 44
  Mildred P. 56
  Susan 56
  William 56

CAMPER
  Infant 67
  Mary Christian 4
  William [Rev.] 4

CANADAY
  A.A. 48
  Alice R. 30
  Lulu V. 48
  V.H. 48

CANIDAY
  Mary 52

CARPENTER
  Anna E. 39
  Annie Laws Ashton 97, 98
  Frances J. 4
  Horace T. 39
  R. E. 4
  Ralph Lester 98
  Sarah E. 4

CARR
  Helen M. 4

CARSON
  Frank 73

CARTER
  Ann 4
  Anne 4
  Aunts 56
  Cousins 56
  E. M. 45
  Georgia 93
  John 56
  M.A. 17, 18

CARTER
  Owner, Tatum Cemetery 90
  Robert M. 45
  Thomas B. 45
  Uncles 56
  W. S. 18

CATLETT
  Kate 4
  Mary 4

CATTERTON
  Emma Jane 57
  George L. 57
  Lelia E. 57
  N. L. 57
  Nimrod P. 57
  S. A. 57
  William W. 57

CAVE
  Agnes Macon 76
  Ann Maria 76
  Benjamin 76
  E. A. 76
  Elizabeth Belfield 76
  Elizabeth Branch 76
  F. H. 76
  Georgianna 76
  Hannah Bledsoe 76
  Isabella deLacy 76
  Lucy Cornelia 76
  Lucy D. 76
  Maria 76
  Maria Cornelia 76
  Mary Frances 76
  Richard 76
  Thomas B.   76
  William Porter 76

CAWTHORNE
  Eliz 83

CHAMBERS
  Harriet 82
  Harvey C. 82
  Kathryn 82
  Mary 17

CHAPMAN
  Mary Stanard 4
  William Henry 4

CHARLES
  Hannah Pidgeon 35, 36
  W. R. 36

CHAUNCEY
  John Francis 99
  Virginia Helena 99

CHESLEY
  Mary Althea 37
  Mary Somerville 37
  William S. 37

CHEWNING
  A.H. 36
  Allie 72
  Madora A. 36
  Sallie Biscoe 39

CHILDRESS
  Giles R. 4
  Lydia J. 30
  Sallie J. 4
  William E. 30

CLARK
 Francis R. 4
 Frank W. 28
 George A. 40
 Guy 44
 Helen M. 4
 J. J. 40
 John William 40
 Joy 40
 Kennie 4
 Lucy 40
 Mildred W. 28
 Minnie Lillian 17
 Susan M. 40
 William Thomas 40

CLARKE
 Beulah Leona 94
 Garland J. 49
 Lena Gertrude 58
 Robert L. 30
 Susan R. 30
 Walter King 58

CLARKSON
 Laura J. 17
 Nancy M. 17

CLAY
 Henry 34

CLAYTON
 Nannie 4

CLOSE
 Louise 92

CLOWES
 Amos K. 17
 Helen V. 17

CLUFF
 Edward 40
 Mary S. 40

COATES
 Margaret H. 17

COLEMAN
 Andrew 95
 Camilta 4
 Edmund Moore 58
 Eva Taylor 58
 Frazier 30
 George W. 60
 Huldah Frazier 37
 John 59
 John Chew 37
 John P. 37
 L. L. 37
 Mary A. 30
 Mr. 62
 Nicholas Penn 37
 plot 11
 T.F. 58
 Thos 58
 Thomas Lafayett 58
 Virginia 95
 Willie Conway 58

COLLINS
 Alice Lucy Yowell 102
 Ann M. 17
 Anne Elizabeth 4
 Eddie L. 102
 Eleanor Davis 17
 James Samuel 17

COLLINS
 Lewis Richard 33
 Lucy D. 17
 R. Frank 102

COLSTON
 Celia 29

COLVIN
 Julia 71
 Melvin 71
 Mr. 61
 W.C. 17

CONFEDERATE SOLDIERS
 Monument 15
 Unknowns 2

CONLEY
 Angeline 17

CONWAY
 Fannie P. 38
 George W. 38
 John Eliason 38
 Lucy H. Macon 73
 Maggie G. 17, 19
 Nellie 4
 P. S. 38
 Reuben 73
COOKE, M. Alice 37
COOPER
 A. H. 40
 Beverly S. 30
 Margaret Jane 40
 Mary A. 34
 Roberta C. 30

COPPAGE
 Mary D. 4

COWHERD
 Adeline R. Harris 17
 E. F. 17
 Ernest H. 17
 Marcellus D. 17
 Mary L. 17
 Norine Victoria 17
 Powell H. 4
 Susan L. 17

COX
 Minnie L. 17

CRANE
 Ethel 85

CREAL
 _____ [father] 28
 Dora 28

CREEL
 Arabella McMullan 17
 Benjamin F. 17

CRENSHAW
 Ines Cusachs 4
 William G. jr 4

CRISP
 Pamela 17

CRITTENDEN
 William 86

CROMPTON
 James 40

CULLEN
 Barbara 4
 George Evans 4

CUNNINGHAM
 Julia 4
 William F. 4

CURTISS
 Dollie 17
 Emma 17
 G.G. 17
 O.B. 17

CUSACHS
 Ines C. 4
 Louise C. 4

DABNEY
 Tyree J. 4
DADE, Genl 98
DALEY
 Alexander 3
 H. W. 5
 John S. 5
 Sarah 5
 Sarah Brent 5

DANDRIDGE
 Mary V. 17
 William B. 17

DANIEL
 Cornelia 17
 J. M. 67
 Matilda Willeroy 5
 Mildred A. 67
 Sarah Travers 17, 19

DARGAN
 Edwin Charles 63
 Ethel Forester 63
 John Herbert 63
 Lucy Augusta 63

DAVENPORT
 Ann 17
 John T. 17, 18

DAVIS
 A. A. [Dr.] 18
 A.M. [Mrs.] 41
 Alice 60
 Boots 2
 Catherine E. 60
 Charlotte S. 36
 Edith Elizabeth 42
 Eliza J. 60
 Elizabeth W. 18
 Eugenia Lambert 60
 F.C. 60
 Fannie C. 60
 Flora Woodward 60
 G.L. [Rev.] 42
 G. T. [Rev.] 41
 George Coleman 60
 Helen McIntosh 32
 Isaac 74
 J. L. 60
 James Edward 60
 James L. 60
 James M. 60
 James Taliaferro 60
 Janet Baker 60
 Jefferson [Pres.] 91, 92
 John A.G. 41
 John W. 18

DAVIS
Laura S. 36
Lewis S. 36
M. C. 60
Margaret 7
Mary 60, 74
Mary W. 5
May Phillips 18
Octavia 5
P. B. 37
Russell Conway 60
Sarah 18
Sarah A. 18
Thomas 60
Thomas J. 59
Thomas Russell 60
Thomas W. 60
Virgil R. 59
William Dudley 18
William J. 18
William T. 18

DAWSON
Child 61
John Carter 28
Lutie Dill 28

DAY
Mrs. 54

DECKER
Alexina Frazer 37
Apphia Ellen 37
M. E. 37
Mary Somerville Chesley 37
Richard C. 37
Walker John 37

deLACY
Isabella 76

DEMPSEY
Albert Sidney 47
Archie A. 47
Arthur S. 47
David A. 47
Nancy E. 47

DENNIS
Charles Henry 100
James M. 5
Sallie Scott 100

DENTON
Mary 18

DESJARDINS
Jeannine 74
Rene C. 74

DETTOR
Jos 18
Lillian A. 18
M. A. 18
Margaret 18
W.F. 18

DEWEY
Annie 30

DICKENSON
Fannie Morton Halsey 64
Florence 5
James 64
Jane 18

DILL
Lutie 28

DOBYNS
Patsy Jean 5

DODD
Sarah 18

DOLIN
Elizabeth M. Stuckdell 18
Johnnie R. 18
Thomas 18, 25

DONAHUE
Genevieve 79

DORFMEYER
Children 85

DOUGLASS
Ardema 58
Eugenia M. 61
Eva Margaret 61
Francis E. 61
Lena Gertrude 58
R.D. 58
Selena M. 61

DOUGLESS
Henry 18

DOVEL
E.G. 18
E. S. 18
George D. 18
J. C. 18
L. W. 18
Mary J. 18

DOWELL
Berryman 18
J. M. 18
Lemuel 18
Lillian A. 18
Lutie J. 18
Margaret 18
Marietta 18
Susan Catherine 18
Tazewell Franklin 18
William L. 18

DOWNER
Carrie Maude 18
Lucy M. 18
Mollie 18, 27
W.W. 18
William R. 18
Willie McMullan 18

DUCKER
Mr. 88

DUDLEY
Rosa B. 52

DULANEY
Catherine H. 56

DULIN
Amelia Roberta 36
J. A. 36
Maggie 36

DUNAWAY
Mariette 28

DUNCAN
Amelia 28
James 28
William 28

DUNN
Ada 18
B. F. [Dr.] 18
Cora 18
F.W. [Lt.] 18
Ida 18
Laura Jane Sale 5
Maria 18
Mary S. 18, 19
lot 17, 19, 24
Scott 18
William H. 5
William M. 18, 19

DUNNINGTON
Gray 76

DUVAL
Jack J. 56, 61, 63
Maria Theodora Cammack 40
Robert Alexander 40

EAHEART
Benjamin T. 54

EARLY
Ida Kingman 19

EARNEST
Betsy Hord Taylor 90, 91
Edmund Taylor 91
Joseph 90, 91
Josephine 91

EAST
Willie 28

ECKLOFF
Josephine E. 5
lot 14
Mary L. 5
R. G. 5

EDDINS
Charlotte J. 19
Henry Clay 17, 19
Richard Oscar 19
Sarah Ellen Marshall 19
Sarah Travers Daniel 19

EDENTON
Edward Ellis 52

EDWARDS
Clementine Simpson 34
Nathaniel J. 34

EGGLESTON
Elnora Virginia 19
R. I. 19

ELEAR
Helen 5, 11

ELENDER
Mattie 19

ELIASON
Susan 38
William E. 38
William P. 80

ELLIOTT
Mary A. 19

ELLIS
Caroline Homassel Barbour
51

ELLIS
    Clara 19

ERIKSEN
    Louise Close 92

ESKEW
    Mary Frances 5
    Walter J. 5
    William J. 5

ESTES
    Annie Cordelia 5
    Blanche Talley 19
    Joseph Hamet 5
    Julia G. 5
    Sallie Minor 5

ETCHISON
    Fannie 19

EUBANK
    George F. 19
    Mary I. H. 60

EUSTACE
    Elizabeth 87

EVANS
    Annie Norvill 19
    James A. 19
    Virginia Taylor 19, 21

FABER
    Ann M. 19
    Annie Belle 19
    Bettie J. 19
    John G. 19
    John W. 19
    Lewis Joel 19
    Mary Lucy Jordan 19
    Minnie Lillian 19
    Sallie A. 19

FARISH
    Mary E. 58
    W. P. T.   58

FARRAR
    Florida 5
    Patsy Atkins 5

FARRER
    Martha Matilda 5
    Robert James 5

FAULCONER
    Benjamin 75
    Edward Jackson 19
    Erasmus G. 5
    James William 40
    Lillie E. Reynolds 40
    Malinda 36
    Mamie 39
    Maria Louise Allan 19
    Mary Anne Massey 75
    Mattie J. 5
    W. Taylor 39
    Willard

FELDMAN
    Tom 62

FERGUSON
    Marjory B. 45

FINCH
    Arthur Lee 85
    Glen Allen 85

FITZGERALD
    Effie D. 47

FITZHUGH
    Francis Conway 17, 19
    John Stuart 32
    Maggie G. Conway 19
    Susan Pannill 32

FLEWELLEN
    Majjp 19

FOULKS
    Harry P. 42
    Lavina P. 42
    William H. 42

FOX
    John T. 5

FRANKLIN
    Ben [Rev.] 12
    Charlotte 5
    Edwin Abbott 101
    Grace Wyatt 101

FRAZER
    Alexina 37
    David McCoy 37
    Don 37
    Emily Irene 37
    Herndon [Rev.] 37
    John 37
    Laura 37
    Lucy 37
    Martha L. 37
    Susan Morton 37
    William S.37

FRAZIER
    Huldah 37

FRENCH
    James Strange 19
    Laura 19
    Laura George 19

FRY
    Mary O. 2, 5
    Philip Henry 2, 5

FUNKHOUSER
    June 92

GAINES
    Andrew 5
    Andrew B. 5
    Frances Lee 5
    George A. 5

GARDNER
    Alexander 30
    Elizabeth A. 30
    Emily J. Waugh 95
    George Morgan 95
    J. M. 95
    James Monroe 5
    Mary Ella 5
    Myrtle 95

GARNETT
    Irene 99

GARNETT
    Jesse W. 5
    Luther L. 5
    Martha C. 5
    Mary E. 5
    Robert C. 5
    Willis D. 5

GARRETT
    ——— 6

GARRISON
    Ann 19
    R. Q. 19
    Sarah E. 19

GARTH
    Martha 6

GAY
    L. [Mrs.] 19

GENTRY
    Bettie E. 6
    Charles H. 6
    Lottie Lee 19
    S.J. 19, 21
    Sarah 19, 21

GEORGE
    Laura 19

GIBBS
    Elizabeth 56

GIBSON
    Ammarilous 6
    Jane Moore 22
    Joseph M. 6
    Linnes Churchill 6
    Nettie J. 6
    William 6
    William Edward 6

GILBERT
    Lavenia Harriet 19

GILES
    Agnes 29

GILLUM
    Sallie Mundy 6
    Thaddeus Oscar 6
    Thos Mann 34

GIPSON
    Benjamin Franklin 6

GODWIN
    Charles 6

GOLSAN
    Charlotte Belle 6
    Edward Nalle 6
    Eustace F. 6

GOOCH
    Helen 19
    Minnie A. 40
    William E. 40

GOODLOE
    Charlotte J. Eddins 20
    E. M. 20
    J. G. 20
    John Robert 20

GOODLOE
Spotswood H. 20

GOODWIN
Caroline D. 37
Charles Edward 78
Harry Wallace 20
John 20
John W. 37
Lucy A. 20
Mary 78
Mary A. 20
Mary E. 20
Nannie A. 20, 21
P. Marvin 20
Sarah Margaret Mason 78
Susie May Baughan 20

GORDEN
Sarah 29

GORDON
Irene Garnett 99
Irene Woodford 99
J. E. 55
James 20
John Addison 63
Lou Brown 55
Lucy 20, 89
Mary 99
Sallie Willis 99

GOSNELL
Lydia 6

GOSS
Ann Carter 6
Ebenezer 6
Mary Botts 6

GOULDMAN
J. R. 44
Virginia 44

GRADY
Alice 69

GRAHAM
David 6
Lizzie Cullen 6
Mary Waterman 6
Robert N. 6
William 6

GRASTY
James D. 30
John Thomas 6
Mary Elizabeth Sale 6

GRAVES
C. Eudora 20
Charles Hubert 64
Emma C. 56
Francis Edward 6
Joseph W.C. 6
Lucy Augusta 64
Martha Ann Hiden 64
Mary Peach Hamilton 6
Mary Virginia 6
Susan Catherine 6
Ursula Kendall 6
Wilhelmina G. Welch 6
William Crittenden 64
William Preston 64

GRAY
Ella 30

GRAY
Fannie 6
Isabella deLacy Cave
      Thompson 76
Leslie Belfield 76
Leslie H. 76

GREENE
John L. 45
John Peyton 45
M. Genevieve 45

GREINER
Christopher C. 20
Roberta J. Watts 20

GRIMES
Genevieve Peyton 45
J. Lee 45
Kate Catlett 6
Peyton 6

GRYMES
Benjamin 6
Benjamin Andrew 6
Bettie Braxton 6
Edward Beale 6
Fannie Gray 6
Fannie Stanard Bradbury 6
Harriet Beale 6
J. Edgar 88
Louis Bull 6
Nannie Clayton 6
Sadie 6

GULLEN
George 41
Louis W. 41
M. S. 41

HACKNEY
Richard 41

HALL
Florence Virginia Loyd 71
Jane L. 20
Joseph Hastin 20
Livie W. 20
Nannie A. 20
Sallie Walton 20
Walton 20

HALSEY
Eloise Rice Walker 7
Fannie D. 64
Fannie Morton 64
Fannie Rice 7
Franklin Stearns 64
Irena Louisa 64
James 64
Joseph J. 7
Mildred J. Morton 7
R. Ogden 7

HAMILTON
Jeanie 45
Mary Peach 7

HAMM
Francis S. 7
Jesse Buel 7
Olga B. 7
Susan G. 7

HAMMOND
Henry R. 7

HANSBOROUGH
Alexander Hamilton 41

HANSBROUGH
John Strother 7
Mary Ballard 7
Mary Elizabeth 7

HANSON
Clarinda 83
Rebecca 53

HARIS
see HARRIS

HARLIN
Mary S. 7

HARLOW
Dan H. 74
James C. 7
John W. 16, 20
Zulemma H. Morris 20

HARNSBERGER
John William 7
Mary S. Harlin 7

HARRELL
Nannie Brockman 44
Theodore Leith 44

HARRIS
Adeline R. 20
Charles M. 30
B.H. 75
Imogene 79
Lucy M. 20
Margaret Victoria 30
Mrs. 53
Richard H. 20

HARRISON
Cassius A. 20
Clara G. 20
George Fisher 20
Nannie 7

HART
Elizabeth H. 20
Jane F. 91
John 91
Thomas W. 20

HARTZOG
Louise E. 52

HATCH
_____ 42
Eugene B. 40
Henry 42
Mary L. 40
Thomas J. 40
Willie H. 40

HATCHER
Gillie Frances Jones 7
Gillie Frances 7
Hillary E. [Rev.] 7

HAYDEN
Joe 65

HEFLIN
_____ 65
Cornelius 20

HENDERSON
Eliza 20
John Uriel 60
Monument 45
HENDRICKS
C. P. 7
Charles Plumb 7
M.N. 7
Margaret N. Davis 7
HERNDON
Amanda L. 36
Claude 36
David C. 65
E.F. 36
Hannah 65
Infant 36
Jessie 36
John B. 40
Lucy 65
Lucy Apperson 65
Lucy Sleet 36
Mary Ann 66
Richard A. 36
Sarah E. 40
William A. 42
HERRING
Ammarilous Gibson 7
Franklin Towles 7
HICKS
Lucy M. 47
Peter Wesley 47
William B. 42
HIDEN
Henry sr 7
Lucy Hiden 73
Martha Ann 64
Mary 7
HIGGINS
George W. 7
HILL
Alice 94
George W. 52
Mary A. 52
HILLS
Dennis 20
Eliza Henderson 20
Thomas Johnson 20
HINTON
Susie E. 52
HOFFMAN
_____ 71
HOGAIN
Mary P. 20
HOLLADAY
Elizabeth Minor 45
Fannie 45
Frances Porter 45
Henry Thompson 45
James Porter 45
Julia Minor 45
Lewis Littlepage 45
Mary Isabelle 45
Mary Love Minor 45
W. T. 45
Waller Lewis 45

HOOKER
Ann Davenport 20
HOPKINS
Harriet 44
Jane J. 44
Marshall 44
Zebulon 44
HOUSEWORTH
B. H. 7
Harriet M. 7
Joseph H. 7
Mary E. 7
Mary Martha 7
Sarah Brent 7
V.A. 7
HOWARD
Charles P. 64
Jane Taylor 64
HUBBARD
Daniel 7
David M. 7
Eugene Winthrop 7
Lydia C. 7
Mary K. 7
Oliver 7
HUCKSTEP
James Edward 20
HUDGINS
George W. 30
Susie M. 30
HUGHES
Mary Ann Herndon 66
Mary E. 44
Mary Jane 20
Mildred 101
Nannie 7
Virginia Louise 66
Wyatte Jefferson 66
HUGHSON
Elizabeth L. 20
HUME
Albert W. 69
Benjamin Wesley 8
Carrie Lee 69
Charles W. 69
David 69
Fanny L. 69
Frances E. 69
Francis 69
John Randolph 39
Lewis W. 39
Lizzie 88
Louisa V.S. 69
Maggie Caldwell 8
Martha B. 39
Mary 69
Mary E. 69
Negro Servants 69
Nora L. Johnson 68
Sarah Ann 69
W.W. [Dr.] 69
William Waller 69
HUNDLEY
_____ Garrett 8
HUNTON
Inez 8

HURKAMP
Alice 8
HURLOCK
Jacob H. sr 48
Laura M. 48
HUTCHINSON
Christopher 8
Elizabeth 8
HUTCHISON
Bradshaw Clarkson 8
Bula Lewis 8
Helen Garret 8
Maude 8
Robert Leachman 8
HUTT
Laura French 20
William Harvey 20
INMAN
Mary 85
"C.V.J." 26
"G.J." 26
"J.F.J." 26
"M.T.J." 26
JACKSON
Barbara 87
Jane G. 66
Joe 66
Joseph S. 67
Mary 67
Preston 87
Stonewall's Arm 70
Tabby Smith 87
William 8
JACOBS
Alice Blanche 8
Ann 30
J. Wallace 8
John Francis 8
Lelia 99
Mary V. 8
JAFFRAY
Florence 8
JAMES
Ann 47
J. W. 40
Kathryn Chambers 82
Lucy S. Keith 40
JEFFERY
Martha L. 21, 26
JEFFRIES
Mary M. 40
JENKINS
Edwin Wyatt 45
JENNINGS
Ada C. 91
Robert A. 47
Willie J. 47
JERDONE
Catherine Robinson 67
Eliza Mayo 67
Francis III 67
Frank 67

JERDONE
Frank 8
Infant 67
John 67
Lillie Robinson 67
Talitha Catherine 8
Walter Peyton 67
William M. 67

JOHNSON
Ann James 47
Bettie P. 48
Carey 78
Clyde 53, 54, 59, 65, 89, 92,93
David 90
Ella 68
Elmira E. 8
Eva 48
Evelyn 8
Fannie 8
G. S. 68
Georgiana Cave 76
Homassel Brown 55
Irving 48
J. Madison 48
J. T. 55
James I. 68
John W. 42
Joseph Henry 8
Lelia 8
Louise K. 42
Lucy Maria 51
Maggie French 78
Mary Elizabeth ,68
Nancy 90
Nora L. 68
Peter T. 76, 90
Philip 43
Robert F. 68
Wallace 8
William M. 68

JONES
Ann Barbara 45
Children 36
Churchill 36
Earl Ray 68
Edmonia Pilcher 8
Gillie Frances 8
H. Broaddus 38
H.P. 38
Juanita 68
L.A. 38
Laney 45
Maggie 28
Martha 45
Mary Ann 66
Mary Ann King 36
Nelson 68
Rufus 48
Wallace [Mrs.] 77
William A. 66

JORDAN
Bettie May 21
Susie A. 19, 21
W.H. 21

JURGESEN
Holger W. 46

KEEFE
Lenora 97, 99

KEELING
Ella 40

KEITH
Lucy S. 40

KENDALL
F. M. 38
Isabelle 38
Ursula 8

KENNEDY
Albert 69
Alice Grady 69
Barbara A. 69
Caroline E. 69
Dora 69
Edgar Sumter 69
Eliza Peyton 69, 99
Ellen M. 69
Ida Smith 69
Jas F. H. 69, 99
Lucy A. 69
Matilda 69
Negro Servants 69
Nellie 69

KENNON
William 21

KEYS
Charles M. 21
Ethel A. 21
Katey 21
M.D. 21
S.M. 21

KEYSER
Ella May Bowen 21
Josephine Elizabeth 21
Oscar Lee 21
William Hampson [Rev.] 21

KIBLER
Eliza A. 8
John H. 8

KING
G.A. 21
Infant 21
L.M. 21
Mary Ann 36

KINZER
Eunice J. 8
John H. 8
Susan C. 8

KITE
_____ 10

KNIGHTON
Anna K. 36
Estelle 36
Grace Irene 40
John T. 36
Mabel 40
Roderick H. 40

KOBLER
Rev. 97

KUBE
Catherine E. 42
Elmer 82
Gertrude 83
John B. 42
William 21

KUPER
C.H. 47

KUPER
Charles L. 47
Mary Ella 47
T. Hunter 47
Virgie H. 47
William C. 47

LACY
William Jones 47

LAMB
Ruby 87

LANCASTER
Adaline T. 36
Ella S. 36
George E. 36
Joseph M. 36
Lucian T. 35, 36
Mary E. 36
Mrs 78
Nellie R. Cammack 36
Richard O. 36
William T. 36

LANDRUM
Huldah 100
Mary 100

LANG
Virginia 98

LARMAND
Maria F. 79

LAWS
Mary 99

LAWSON
Pearl 101
Sarah 101
Welford 101

LEAKE
Eva Lena 21
F. Carter 21
F.M. 21
Lena 21
Sarah E. West 21

LEE
Ambrose Madison 73
Edward 44
Eliza Massey 75
Elizabeth 91, 92
Fannie 74
Frances 8
Hancock 91
John Wills 73
Lafayett 75
Lottie 2, 19
Lucy C. 73
Mary W. 73
Richard 91
Susan 44
William Harvey 40

LEWIS
Annie 8
Cora 98
David 70
Huldah 46
Nellie 97

LINNEY
Charles Beale 21
Henry Bascom 19, 21
Henry Marshall 21

LINNEY
  James Harrington 21
  Lucy Gordon 21
  Virginia Taylor Evans 21

LIPSCOMB
  Charlie D. 8
  Claborn 8
  Harry E. 8
  J. Thomas 8
  John 8
  Lizzie G. 8
  Mary E. 8
  Miles B. 8
  Millie B. 8
  Octavia M. 8
  Rich W. 8
  Robert 41
  Robert M. 9
  Rosa L. 9
  Virginia L. 9

LOCKER
  George 21
  Lillian Synan 21

LOCKHART
  J.E. "Jim" 21
  John A. 21
  Margaret 21
  Martha M. 21
  Martha Miller 21
  Samuel 21
  William M. 21

LOYD
  Cassandra Paxton 21
  Florence Virginia 71
  Jane Moore Gibson 22
  Thos E. 22

LUCAS
  Alice 45, 46
  Ernest 72
  Julie 72

LUCK
  Ella S. 44
  William A. 44

LUCKETT
  L.J. 46
  L.T. 46
  Lucie P. 46
  Thornton 46

LUMSDEN
  Ann Jacobs 30
  Annie A. 30
  Charlie L. 72
  E. Frank 72
  E. J. 30
  Henry Clay 72
  Inez I. 72
  Infants 30
  James Fife 30
  John R. 72
  Matilda H. 72
  Mary L. 72
  Sarah F. 30
  Vernon O. 72

LUSHWAY
  Juliet R. 21
  Peter 21

LYNCH
  Mary Inman 85
  William Anderson 85

LYNN
  Andrew J. 20, 21
  Mary Frances 21
  Milton 21
  Nannie A. Goodwin 21

"A.E.M." 26
"E.S.M." 26

MACDONALD
  Amy B. 72
  Angus Avery 72, 77
  Angus Snead 72, 77

MACON
  Emma Cassandra Riley 9
  J. Madison 9, 73
  Lucetta T. Newman 9, 73
  Lucy H. 73
  Reuben Conway 9
  Sarah G. 73
  Thomas 73

MADDUX
  Charlotte Langhorne Butler
        9
  Clifford Bartlett 9
  Marie 9

MADISON
  Alfred 73
  Ambrose 73
  Ambrose G. 73
  Dolley Payne 73
  Fannie W. 73
  James [Pres.] 73, 91, 92
  James 73
  James A. 73
  Letitia R.L. 73
  Lucy M. 73
  R.L. [Dr.] 73
  Susan Daniel 73

MAHANES
  Emily V. 21
  Frances E. 21
  Samuel Gariet 21
  Tavner O. 21

MALLORY
  David G. 78

MANLEY
  Annie E. 21
  G.H. 21
  James L. 21
  Robert F. 21, 26
  Sallie E. Via 21, 22

MANN
  Annie Cleveland 40
  Arabella B. 22
  Estelle Jamie 40
  Jas J. 40
  Mabel E. 40
  Sara J. 40
  Talbot G. 22
  W.H. 22

MANSFIELD
  Cassandra Paxton 22
  Thos N. 22

MARKS
  Eliza S. 22

MARQUIS
  Martha G. 9
  Walter Albert 9

MARRIETT
  Angelina M. 22

MARRINER
  Julia Wilson 22

MARSH
  E. H. 22

MARSHALL
  Annie L. 9
  B.J.'s Bismark 75
  Charles H. 19
  Elizabeth J. 75
  Fielding Lewis 9
  John W. 75
  Mary Newton 9
  Mary W. Davis 9
  Sallie A. Faber 22
  Sarah Ellen 22
  Winfield N. 9

MARTIN
  Alfred 39
  Edmonia 44
  Elizabeth P. 44
  Emma J. 44
  Henry K. 44
  Hollis R. 44
  Jane Dickinson 22
  Josephine C. 44
  Katie 39
  Lewis A. 44
  Lissie May 44
  Lucy A. 39
  Mary 22
  Mary B. 9
  Mattie Elender 22
  Oliva C. 44
  Patrick 22
  W.J. 44
  Warren D. 44
  William Elmore 44
  William H. 22, 44

MARYE
  Mary F. 73

MASON
  Lynea J. 22
  Sallie E. 36
  Sarah Margaret 78
  W.T. 36
  Wyle Charles [M.D.] 74

MASSEY
  Asa J. 75
  Coosa Roberta 75
  Eliza 75
  John Hansford 75
  Mary Anne 75
  Oscar Gillispie 75
  Sally Ann 75

MATTHEWS
  Martha 34
  William 34

MAY
  Herman 71, 85

MAY
Mary Francis 9

MAYHUGH
Coffer 22

MAYO
Eliza 67

McALISTE
John T. 22

McALISTER
Sarah E. 38
Thomas C. 28
Verona L. 28
W.B. 38

McALLISTER
Virgie 22, 26

McCALL
C. Cadoza 29

McCLARY
Charles L. 46
James Garland 46
Lucy V. 46
Musa Dora 46
Rachel Bledsoe 46

McCORD
Cornelia 40
Daniel G. 40
Jacob S. 44
Samuel A. 40
Susie 40

McDANIEL
Madison 28

McDONALD
John 9
Marshall C. 9
Mettie 9

McELROY
Samuel B. 22
Sarah Bausman 22

McGEHEE
Aldia 101
Andrew J. 101
Charles R. 101
Eddie J. 101
George C. 101
M. W. 22
Mabel C. 101
Maggie 101
Manna 101
Mary 101, 102
Mary E. 22
Mildred A. Hughes 101
Resa 101
Ruth 101
Thomas J. 102
William 102

McILWAINE
A. G. 22
J. H. 22
Sammie 22

McINTOSH
Cora 32
Ebbie Frank 9
Helen 32

McINTOSH
Infant sons 9
James 32
Mary Eliza Perry 9
Myra N. 9
Nancy 9
Phyllis 9
William [Rev.] 33

McMULLAN
Arabella 22
Lynn B. [Capt.] 20
Mary Jane Hughes 22
Maude Trevanian 22
Omer 22
Virginia 22
Willie 22

McMURRAN
A.S. 22
Charles 22
Jane Peter 22
M. V. 22

McVEIGH
Martha A. 9

MICHIE
Sarah T. 34

MILLER
A.J. 9
Leslie Glen 55
Martha 22
Mary Ellen 22
Virginia McMullan 22

MINOR
John 46
John Bailey 46
Mary Love 46
Sallie 9

MITCHELL
Mattie 22

MODENA
Alice 75
Bettie 76
B. J. 76
B. S. 76
Charles H. 76
Infant 76
James William 76

MONCURE
Annie Lewis 9
Charles Proser 9
Elizabeth Randolph 9
Henry 9
Peter V.D. 9
Sadie Grymes 9

MOORE
Charles H. 77
Charles W. 77
Edgar 77
Eleanor P. 77
Elizabeth 22
Ella 32
James Mordecai 9
James Stapleton 9
Mollie V. 77
Virginia B. 77
Virginia Margaret Sale 9
William W. 102
Willmonia Endora 9

MORRIS
Addie E. 48
Ann Louisa 9
Fenton 9
Great-grandfather 77
Great-grandmother 77
Hampden Pleasants 23
J. B. 16
J. E. sr 9
James Harrison 48
John L. 48
Julia M. Bickers 23
Lemuel 23
Lula 9
Milton 9
Zaidee 23
Zulemma H. 23

MORTON
Alice H. 9
Emily D. 9, 10
George [Dr.] 89
George W. 38
J. Kemper 10
James W. 9, 10
Laura Frazer 38
Lucy P. 10
Mildred J. 10
Sallie 40
Susan 38
Susie Laura 38
William 60, 77

MUNDY
Burrus 78
____Lancaster 78
Mary Goodwin 78
Philip [Mrs.] 78
Sallie 10

MURPHY
George 23
H.S. 23
James Mason 22
Magdalene B. 51
Mary Ellen Miller 23
Myrtle Shirley 79

NALLE
Lucy Mary 10
Sarah Ellen 100

NELSON
Eleanor Taliaferro 10
Octavia Davis 10
R. Lewis 10

NEWMAN
Ann Marie Blakey 10
Bettie B. 10
Catherine Randolph
Taylor 23
Conway 23, 26
Cora A. 79
Eleanor 23
Eleanor Taylor 23
Florence 23
Genevieve Donahue 79
Imogene Harris 79
J. Sheridan 23
James 23
John F. 10
John R. 79
Lucetta Todd 9, 10, 73
Lucy 79
Margaret Rogers 79
Mary S. 23

NEWMAN
Mildred E. 23
Nannie B. 23
Nannie Wirt 23
Nathaniel Welch 23
Reuben M. 23
Sara Martha 98
Sarah 60
Sallie J. 23
Tho 60
William 79
William Q. 79
Willie Ann 98

NEWTON
Mary 9

NEY
Nannie 10

NOBLE
Alice V. Riley 23
John A. 23

NOON
Susie B. 23, 26

NORQUIST
Edith 74

NORVILL
Annie 23

NOTTINGHAM
Sally B. 10

OAKES
Thomas M. 36

ODEN
Lewis Thomas 10

OGG
Lydie F. 23

OWENS
Margaret 94

PALMER
Leonard S. 23
Mary Jane 23
Nora 95

PANNILL
Alice S. 80
Annie P. 80
Blanche 80
Charlotte L. 39
Dannie F. 80
David 60
Delia C. 80
Fannie B. 80, 95
Fannie Bruce 80
G. Morton 80
George M. 80
George W. 39
Harry Lee 80
Infant 80
J. W. 80
Joseph B. 80, 95
Lee 80
Mattie Porter 80
Phillip P. 80
Phillip Payne 80
Robert Dandridge 80
Susan 32

PARKER
Alice 10
D. [Rev.] 29
George Samuel 10
Inez Hunton 10

PARRAN
Mary Virginia Graves 10
William S. 10

PARROTT
Lucy Jane 23

PATTERSON
Angelina M. Marriett 23
Clementine W. 25
I. 23
Willie 23, 25

PAULI
Mary Eliza 97, 99

PAXTON
Cassandra 23

PAYNE
Anne Elizabeth Collins 10
Benjamin C. 10
Cecil 23
Charles 48
Dolley 73
Elizabeth C. 48
Eliza J. T. 48
George A. 23
James M. 34
James T. 48
Magnus 23
Mary Elizabeth 34
Mary Shadrach 48
Mattie 94
Maury 23
William H. 48

PENDLETON
Betty 96
Frances 91

PEREGORY
Infant 60
Sarah 60

PERRY
Archibald 10
Children 10
Elijah Richard 44
George L. 44
Julia A. 10
Julia A. Mundy 10
Levi L. 10
Mary [Polly] Brown 44
Maude 10
Robert Lee 10
Rudolph 10
Sophia S. Boston 44
Tomasia Myrtle Bickley 44

PETER
Jane 23

PEYTON
Alice H. 46
Anna Dade 97, 99
Cora Lee 97
Eliza 69, 99
Genevieve 46
George O. 46

PEYTON
George Washington 97, 98
Georgiana 98
Henry Llewellyn 97, 99
Huldah Lewis 46
Infants 97
James Franklin 98
John 97
John S. 46
John Stigler 98
John W. 46
Lenora Keefe 97
Lucy F. 97, 98
Lydia Price Snyder 97,
    99
Mary Eliza Pauli 97
Mary Jane 97, 98
Sallie B. 10, 97
Sarah Martha 46, 98
Thomas J. 10, 97, 99
Willa Anna 46
William S. 46, 98
Willie Ann Newman 98
Willie Lewis 46

PHILLIPS
Camilla C. 23
John Swift 23
John Wilmer 23
Joseph N. 23
May 23
Reuben 32
Rosa B. 23
Virginia H. 32

PIDGEON
Hannah 36
Mary Jane 36

PIERCE
Patsey 28

PILCHER
Edmonia 10

PINKARD
Mary Ann 38

PORTER
Frances 46
John A. 80
Mary A. M. 23
Mary C. 23, 80
Mattie 80
William Henry 23

POWELL
C.G. 57
Charles LeVert 57
Hattie H. 57
Henry 86
Lelia E. 57
Lillie Olivia 31
Sarah E. Carpenter 10
Susan J. 57
W. N. 10

PRESSLEY
J. H. [Rev] 43

PRICE
David [Capt.] 10
Walter Evan Esq. 10

PRIEST
Albert Tellous 95

PRIEST
  Eleanor 95
  Mary E. 95
PROCTOR
  Mildred H. Bledsoe 24
  Orlander 24
PUGH
  Ada C. Jennings 91
  Caroline McNeill 91
  John W. 91
QUANN
  Anna C. 82
  David 82
  G. Melvin 82
  Gracy May 32
  Hugh W. 82
  Infant 82
  J. H. 32
  John William 82
  M. E. 32
  Mary 82
  Rebecca F. 82
  Sarah Catherine 82
  Tacy A. 82
  William H. 82
QUARLES
  Lucy 90
  William 90
QUESENBERRY
  A.B. 10
  Vivian [Dr.] 10
QUISENBERRY
  Benjamin 31
  Bettie E. 38
  Daniel 31
  Elizabeth 31
  G.W. 31
  S.C. 31
RANDOLPH
  Charles 41
  Mary 41, 94
  Roberta M. 41
  Wallace 94
RAWLINGS
  Benjamin sr 10
  Martha A. McVeigh 10
  Zachariah Herndon 10
REED
  Mille 29
REEDY
  Camilta Coleman 11
  John A. 11
REID
  Albert 28
  Eliza Ellen 11
  Eugenia 28
  Hiram G. 11
  Sheldon A. 11
REVELEY
  Edmund Pendleton 91
  Graham 91
  Mildred Turner 91
  Robinette Taylor 91
  Thomas 91

REYNOLDS
  Alville 83
  Charles Alfred 31
  Eliza 31
  Ella G. 31
  Estelle Irine 31
  George Washington 31
  Jenera 31
  Lillie 40
  Lucy Frances Rhoades 83
  Maretta J. 31
  Richard Morton 24
  Sarah Dodd 24
RHOADES
  Archilles 42
  Baby 95
  Catherine E. Kube 42
  Clarinda Hanson 83
  Elizabeth Cawthorne 83
  George W. 24
  Gertrude Kube 83
  Gillie M. 85
  J. L. V. 24
  John 83
  L.A. [Mrs.] 95
  Lilly Mann 24
  Lucy Frances 83
  Lucy Wright 83
  Nancy 42
  P. 24
  R. Wayne 48
  Rebecca Hanson 83
  Richard 83
  Richard Benjamin 83
  Robert [Mrs.] 49, 77
  Samuel 85
  Susan Rhoades 83
  William Richard 83
RICE
  Ella 7, 11
RICHARDS
  Huey 79, 96
RICHARDSON
  Anne Yeates 11
  Barbara Cullen 11
  Edward H. sr 84
  George Dudley 11
  Martha E. 91
  Mary L. 43
  Tucker 84
RICKARD
  Emma C. 11
  William H. 11
RIDER
  Lizzie 67
RIELY
  Catherine Brent 9
  Emma Cassandra 11
  James Purvis 9
RILEY
  Alice V. 24
RINER
  Adeline A. 24
  Edgar M. 47
ROACH
  Annie Florence 84

ROACH
  John Lewis 84
ROBERTS
  Edgar 94
  Fannie Robertson 11
  Infant 85
  James Cameron 60
  John A. 11
  Joseph P. 11
  Julia Washington 94
  Lucy M. 11
  Mary Davis 60
  Pleasant D. 11
  Robert 85
  Roger Q. 11
  Thomas J. 11
ROBERTSON
  Ann Eliza 34
  Fannie 11
  J. H. 24
  Richard 34
ROBINSON
  Catherine 68
  Charlotte H. 29
  George 29
  Georgiana Peyton 98
  James 5, 11
  John Jones 98
  Lillie 68
  Louis W. jr 52
  Lucy May 68
  Maria L. 11
  Mary J. 29
  Thomas A. 11
  William T. 24
ROGERS
  _____ 96
  Ada Dunn 24
  Ernest B. 96
  Finella H. 11
  Infant 24
  Margaret 79
  Mary A. 96
  William Samuel 24
ROHR
  Susan Jane 11
  Thomas M. 24
ROLLINS
  Ethel Crane 85
  James A. 85
  James William sr 85
  Mary Alice 85
ROSS
  Nellie 73
ROUTT
  M. E. 24, 26
ROW
  Eliza W. 11
  James W. 41
  Jane B. 41
  John S. 11
ROWE
  E. W. [Dr.] 11
  Ida L. 11
  Mary Elinor 11
  Thomas E. 11

RUNKLE
  George W. 23, 24
  Lydia F. Ogg 24
RUSSELL, Sallie T. 24
SACRA
  Jane Seal 96
  Jesse 96
SALE
  Laura Jane 11
  Mary Elizabeth 11
  Mary Spotswood 11
  R. C. 60
  Virginia Margaret 11
  William Davis 11
SANDERS
  John F. 24
  John R. 48
  Lillian 53
  Lynea J. Mason 24
  Mary A. 48
  Mary Cattlett 53
  Mollie E. 41
  Rebecca Hanson 53
  William Edward Minor 24
  William Preston 41
SANFORD
  Lawrence 86
  Lelia Johnson 11
  Lucy H. 86
  Lulie 86
  Mr. 97
SARGEANT
  H.H. [Dr.] 24
  M.W. 24
  Robert 24
SAUNDERS
  Francis Jones 86
SCHLOSSER
  George William 24
  Mary Belle 24
  Samuel Gough 24
SCOTT
  Anna Pleasants 24
  C. Eudora Graves 24
  Charles 100
  Charles Lee 24
  Charles Poindexter 100
  Claudia Marshall Willis
     24
  Delia 100
  Edmund Willis 24
  Fanny 100
  Garrett 100
  George 100
  Huldah Jane 47, 48
  James Martin 11
  Jane 100
  John 24, 100
  Johnson Daniel 47, 48
  Julia 100
  Marion 100
  Mary 100
  Mary Landrum 100
  Pamelia Augusta 24
  Philip 100
  Rosa Amos 100
  Sallie 100
  Sarah Ellen Nalle 100
  Susan Catherine Graves
     11
  Thomas 100

SCOTT
  William C. 24
  William Wallace 24
  Wyclif 24
SEAL
  Frances 96
  Jane 96
  John W. 11
  Louansy 11
  Rosala 96
SEEDS
  Artford D. 61
  Mary Hildreth 61
  Mary M. 61
  Robert Carroll 61
SEELY
  J. 42
  S. C. H. 42
SELBY
  Benjamin F. sr 11
  Lydia Gosnell 11
SENTZ
  Charles F. 57
  Hattie H. 57
SEYMOUR
  Bessie 24
SHADRACH
  Mary 48
SHAW
  Fannie Stanard 11
  Thomas J. 11
SHEPHERD
  Bettie 24
  James 11, 91
  Lucinda A. Taylor 91
SHIFFLETT
  George D. 87
  George N. 87
  Lillie Florence 87
  Nora C.
  Ruby Lamb 87
  Rufus Jackson 87
SHIRKEY
  Henrietta Louise 98
SIMMONS
  Barbara Jackson 87
  Cyrus 87
SIMMS
  Edmund R. 87
  Edmund Richard jr 87
  Elizabeth 87
  Mattie I. 87
  Oliver 87
SIMPSON
  Clementine 34
  Eliza J. 36
  Hugh M. 36
SIMS
  Anna Kelly 74
  David   74
  Edith Norquist 74
  Lucy A. 12
  Mary Davis 74

SIMS
  Robert Angus 74
  Wilson T. 12
SISSON
  Bessie Blair 69
  Dora Kennedy 69
  Edgar S. 69
  James Russell 69
  John Row 69
  Joseph Quinton 88
  Laura Caroline 88
  Lizzie Hume 88
  Mildred Hannah 88
  Oscar L. 69
SIZER
  J. M [Rev.] 41
  Nellie V. 41
SLAUGHTER
  Alfred E. [Dr.] 12
  Eugenia Taylor 12
  Lester 88
  Mary L. 88
  Mary S. 88
  Mercer 88
  plot 20
  Sidney N. 88
SLEET
  Lucy 36
SMITH
  A. Custis 24
  Annie 95
  Annie Dewey 31
  Annie E. 31
  Clarence 88, 89
  Edgar Daniel 24
  Edna M. 24
  Eliza Boose 28
  Francis M. 31
  George W. 24
  Gladys V. 88
  Ida 69
  James W. 28
  Louisa 89
  Lucy Frances Rhoades
     Reynolds 83
  Lucy Jane Parrott 24, 25
  Luticia 89
  M. A. 24
  M. M. 24
  Marcellus 83
  Mary H. 12
  Mary Hansbrough 12
  Morris Chabels 12
  Mr. 97
  Sarah A. 25
  Tabby 87
  W. J. 12
  W.T. jr 25
  William B. 48
  William J. 12
  William Joseph 24, 25
SMITHERS
  C.H. 25
  Helen Gooch 25
  Howard Sale 25
  James Dowell 25
SNEED
  Clara Ellis 25
  Elizabeth Woolfolk 25
  Ellis Hurt 25

SNEED
John Lafayette 25
Littleton Waller 25
William Henry 25

SNYDER
Lydia Price 97, 98
Martha Stigler 97
Michael 97
Willie 25

SOMERVILLE
Jeanie Hamilton 46
John H. 41
Mary Hamilton 46
plot 15
Samuel Wilson 46
Sarah Elizabeth 41

SORRELL
Charles T. 102
Joseph Allie 102
Maggie McGehee 102

SOUDER
Charles M. 25
Herbert 25
L___w 25

SPARKS
Nannie Harrison 12
Robert W. 12

SPICER
William Earl 93

SPOTSWOOD
Alexander Dandridge 89
Alexander Gordon 89
Lucy Gordon 89
Mary 12

STANARD
Fannie 12
Mary 12

STARRETT
Catherine 25

STEPHENS
Joseph H. 12
Martha 12

STEWART
Catherine 46
William 46

STIGLER
Martha 97

STONESIFTER
F. H. 25
Virginia 25

STOVIN
Bettie B. Newman 12
Charles J. 12
Maude Taylor 12

STRATTON
A.E. 25
George Elmer 25
M. E. 25
R. H. 25
Richard Henry 25

STRICKLER
Harrison 12
John C. 25
Lee K. 25
Mary J. 25
Sarah J. 12

STRONG
Rebecca A. 44
Robert C. 44

STUCKDELL
Elizabeth M. 25

STUNTZ
Minnie L. Cox 25
W. P. 17

SULLIVAN
Cameller 90
Emma 94
Infants 90
Myrtle 94
Walt 64, 94

SUTHERLAND
Ada Z. 36
Richard W. 36
Virginia L. 36

SWAIN
John Henry 44
Mollie W. 44

SWIFT
Elizabeth J. 36

SYME
Robina 46

SYNAN
Lillian 25

TALIAFERRO
Alexander Galt 12
Anthony Barclay 12
C. C. 12
Charlotte Franklin 12
Edmund Pendleton 12,
  13
Eleanor 12
Harriet Bynam Tinsley
  12
Hay 91
James Barbour 51
Jaquelin P. 12
John [Capt.] 12
John Seymour 51
Kathleen Newman 12
Lucy Maria Barbour 51
Lucy Maria 51
Lucy Willis 12
Mary Wilkinson 12
Mildred 91
Octavia Hortense 12, 13
Thomas Garland 12
Victoria T. 12
William Alexander 12
William R. 46

TALLEY
Blanche 25
Fannie A. 46
Malinda B. 44

TATE
_____25

TATE
Addison L. 25
Annie M. 25
E.W. 25
N.E. 25
Willie M. 25

TATUM
Ada B. 90
Lucy 12
Nellie Kennedy 69
Robert H. 90

TAYLOR
Alexander F. 91
Alice E. 25
Allie French 25, 26
Anna W.L. 12
Annie Hestell 25, 26
Barbara 26
Catherine Randolph 26
Charles W. 28
E. Moore 64
Edmund Pendleton 12
Edmund P. 90, 91
Eleanor 23, 26
Elmer C. 26
Erasmus 3, 12, 64, 91
Eva 58
Frances Pendleton 91
George Carter 26
George William 25
Howard 91
Hyrum S. 26
Ida William 26
Isabelle Macnish 91
J. M. 64
James Longstreet 91
James II 92
Jane 64
Jaquelin P. 91
Lucinda A. 91
Lucy Jane 91
Martha E. 91
Mary C. 91
Mary Edmonia 91
Mary Ella 25, 26
Maud 12
Mildred Edmonia 90, 91
Rebecca 28
Robert 91
Robert O. 26
Roberta 3, 12, 91
Robina 46
Robinette 91
Sara Knox 91, 92
Susie B. Noon 26
Virgie McAllister 26
W.J. 25
William G. 46
Zachary 91, 92

TENNANT
David B. 12
Mary W. 12

TERRELL
Buckner 92
Glanville 92
Howard Macaulay 92
Jane S. 92
Junius S. 92
Lucy Ann 92
Mary J. 92
O. H. P. jr 92
Oliver H. P. 92

TERRELL
  Percy T. 92
  Sarah Jerdone 92

TERRILL
  Elizabeth Eustace 87
  Florence Dickenson 12
  Janett 12
  John 87
  Lucy Frazer 38
  Oliver Towles 38
  Robert M.[Dr.] 33
  Susan M. 12, 13
  Towles 12, 13
  Uriel [Dr.] 13
  William Edward Thomas 12,
                13

THAYER
  Angeline K. 41
  John S. 41

THOMAS
  Henry 29
  Nellie D. 52
  Sophia 44

THOMASSON
  G. Frank 26
  George Francis 26
  Jane O. 26
  S. C. 26

THOMPSON
  Ella 85
  Ella Gray 31
  Emma 51
  Infant 85
  Isabella deL. 76
  John G. 31
  Maria Cornelia Cave 76
  Martha Helen 46
  Robert 85
  William Cave 76

THORNTON
  _____ 55
  Alice Thurman 26
  Bennie 26
  Ida Kingman Early 26
  James 46
  James A. 26
  Lucie P. Luckett 46

THURMAN
  Alice 26
  B. F. 26
  M. E. Routt 26

THURSTON
  _____ 54, 93
  Georgia Carter 93
  Reuben 93

TIGNOR
  Florida Farrar 13
  Mildred 13
  Thomas J. 13

TIMBERLAKE
  Chapman 93
  J. W. 60
  Jane 60
  Lucy A. 26

TINDER
  _____ 49, 83

TINDER
  Alice May 31
  Bertha 96
  Ella Keeling 41
  Estelle Irine 31
  Herbert E. 31
  John Spencer 41
  Mildred H. 31
  Thomas T. 31

TINSLEY
  A.H.S. 93
  G.H.T. 93
  Harriet Bynam 13
  Henry E. 93
  H.E.T. 93
  T.A. 93

TOONAN
  Frances Seal 96

TREVANIAN
  Maude 26

TRUMBO
  L.C. 41

TUCKER
  John W. 41
  Mollie H. 41

TUEL
  Issac 13
  J.P. 13

TURNER
  Arthur 72
  Charles E. 94
  Elizabeth Pendleton 91
  H. W. 94
  Mildred Edmonia 92
  Reuben 91
  Sally 72
  Virginia Samuel 26, 27

TWYMAN
  Ettie M. 26

URQUHART
  Charles 63
  Finnelia 63

VAN LEAR
  Permealia M. 46
  Robert 46

VASS
  William P. 38

VAUGHAN
  Henrietta 26
  Pascall 26
  T.W. [Rev.] 29

VERLING
  George Lee 26
  Mildred Ann 26

VIA
  Sallie E. 21, 26

WADDEL
  James 1

WALKER
  Adelia M. 38
  Anne Carter 13

WALKER
  Eliza S. 13
  Eloise Rice 13
  George T. 26
  Henry T. 26
  H. Wellington 26
  James 86
  John S. 13
  John W. [D.D.] 21, 26
  John Weber 26
  Joseph 13
  Marion 86
  Martha L. Jeffrey 26
  Mary S. 86
  Mildred A. 26
  Nannie B. Newman 26
  P.T. 86
  Pollie B. 28
  Robert Stringfellow 13
  Sallie 13
  Susan H. 13
  T.G. 28
  Walter 26
  William J. 26

WALLACE
  Emma Sullivan 94
  Ethel 72
  Festus 94
  Irvin F. 94
  John D. 94
  John R. 94
  Margaret Owens 94
  Thomas P. 13
  Victoria T. 13

WALLER
  Luther B. 39

WALTERS
  G.C. 57
  Keith 51, 93
  P.A. 57

WALTON
  Sallie 26

WAMBERSIE
  Alice Parker 13
  John Edward [Capt.] 13

WARNER
  Helen M. 13
  Mary 13

WARREN
  Harry Innes 13
  Hurkamp Alice 13

WASHINGTON
  _____ 54, 57
  Alverda S. 55
  Chas 33
  John 95
  Judy 33
  Julia 95
  Margaret 95
  Mattie Payne 94
  Roger Lee 95
  Wesley 94

WATERMAN
  Mary 13

WATKINS
  Anne 68
  Edward 68
  James S. jr 18, 27

WATKINS
James S. sr 18, 27
Mary E. 41
Mollie Downer 27

WATSON
Elmer 85
Joab L. 13
Mary Francis May 13

WATTLES
Alvin Morton 98
Andrew Jackson 13
Mary Eliza 13
Nannie Gordon Wilkins 98

WATTS
Roberta J. 20, 27

WAUGH
Bertha Tinder 96
Chas A. 28
Charles S. 95
Charlie 96
Cora L. 95
Ellen C. 41
Emily J. 95
Emma 44
Garrett E. 95
George Morgan 95
Goree 41
Goree E. 95
Jane Frances 44
Mary 95
Nora Lee 95
Nora Palmer 95
Robert Goree 41
Sallie W. 28
Sarah 95

WEAVER
B. Franklin 27
Nellie P. 27

WEBB
A. 86
Alice R. Canady 31
Augustine 27
Benjamin Rosser 36
Betty M. 36
Charles P. 36
Effie 13
F. L. 96
Fannie Vivion 86
Harriet Elizabeth 13
Jane 31
John Arthur 30, 31, 96
Lia 86
Martha J. 42
Sallie E. 36

WELCH
Arria 56
Wilhelmina G. 13

WELCHER
Maude 49

WEST
Martha 29
Sarah E. 27

WEV
Elizabeth N. 27

WHARTON
Charlotte A. 28

WHARTON
Jefferson 28

WHITE
96
John 96

WHITLOCK
Bettie S. 13
Betty 96
Byrd Lee 13
George 13
Grandfather 96
Grandmother 96
Martha M. 13, 96

WILHOIT
Jacob N. 13
John Newton 13
Mariah L. 57
Sarah Elizabeth 13

WILKINS
Cora Lewis 98
George 27
James Edward 99
John Peyton 97
John Quincy Adams 97, 98
Kate May 97
Lucy E.M. 27
Lucy F. Peyton 97, 98
Lucy Virginia 98
Lutta Erwin 98
Magnus Taliaferro 98
Magnus Waite 98
Mary Laws 99
Nannie Gordon 98
Nellie Lewis 97, 98
Virginia Lang 98

WILKINSON
Mary 13

WILLEROY
Matilda 13

WILLIAMS
Emily Brent 13
Evelyn Johnson 14
Evelyn K. 14
Fannie B. 80, 95
Hubert 14
James [Capt.] 89
Mildred Pendleton 14
Richard Catlett 14
Roberta Banks 13, 14
Wesley 29
William Clayton jr 14
William Grymes 13, 14

WILLIAMSON
Joseph A. 42

WILLIS
B.D. 14
Claudia 73
Claudia Marshall 27
Fannie 73, 74
H. L. 14
H. Lee 88
John [Dr.] 74
John 73, 74
John Churchill 99
Larkin 99
Lewis 14
Lucie S. 74
Lucy 74

WILLIS
Lucy Mary 14
Lucy T. 14
Mary 74
Mary E. 73
Mary Gatesby Woodford 99
Mary Gordon 99
Nellie 74, 88
Nellie Conway 14
Richard H. 14
Richard Henry 14
Sallie 99
William Byrd 14

WILLOUGHBY
Arrabella Ann 44, 45
Thomas S. 44, 45

WILSON
Julia 27
Robert 42

WILTSHIRE
Asalea D. 36, 37
Benjamin David 99
Cassie J. 36
Grace E. 36
Jessie O. 36, 37
Joseph A. 14
Lelia Jacobs 99, 100
Malinda Faulconer 37
Martha R. 37
R.L. 36, 37
Sarah Elizabeth 14
Silas P. 37
W.B. 14
Weedon 36, 99, 100

WINN
Mary J. 14
Thomas J. 14

WINSLOW
Frederick W. 14
Martha J. 14

WIRT
Florence Newman 27
Joseph E. 27
Nannie 27

WOLFLEY
John 42
Richard H. 42

WOOD
Arthur C. 101
Caroline 101
David 101
E.M. 27
Fielding 101
George Wilson 101
James Henry 26, 27
Joseph B. 55
Mary E. 101
Preston D. 101
Sidney D. 27
Virginia Samuel Turner 27

WOODFORD
Irene 99
Mary Gatesby 99

WOODRIFF
Florence Jaffray 14
John R.P. 14

WOODWARD
    Flora 60

WOOLFOLK
    Elizabeth 27
    John Lafayette 58
    Sarah C. 58

WORMLEY
    Charles 79

WORSTER
    Arianna 27
    M. J. 27

WRIGHT
    Benjamin 31
    Columbia 31
    Cordelia H. 31
    David [M.D.] 46
    Frederick G. 46
    James 34
    Lizzie E. 47
    Lucy 83
    Lucy C. 14
    Susie 31
    W. Andrew 14

WYATT
    Aldia McGehee 102
    Grace 102
    Homer N. 102
    Jack 101
    Joseph? Jacob? 102
    Joseph Oscar 102
    Manna M. 102
    Nancy T. 102

"Y"
    John T. 51

YAGER
    Charles W. 27
    Jos H. 27
    Sallie D. 27
    Sallie W. 14

YANCEY
    Jane E. 14
    Janett 14
    Jno W. 14
    Sarah M. T. 14

YATES
    George N. 14
    Leo 50
    Margaret P.14
    Snowden 14

YOUNG
    Charles O. 14
    Cornelia E. 27
    James S. 27
    Josie S. 27
    Samuel M. 27

YOWELL
    Alice Lucy 102
    James N. 27
    Mary M. 27

────────
    Lou W. 43

www.ingramcontent.com/pod-product-compliance
Lightning Source LLC
Chambersburg PA
CBHW070925270326
41927CB00011B/2733